Praise for *Creating Luminous Spaces*

"Highly recommended! Maureen Calamia has done an excellent job making the elements of feng shui at once understandable and usable in this carefully researched and thoughtful book. Discovering what element most closely represents your energy can help in so many areas of your life!"
—**Denise Linn**, author of
Sacred Space and *Feng Shui for the Soul*

"Maureen dives deep into understanding how home affects us. She draws on the Five Elements, ancient teachings that let our stories unfold and our conversations about life to begin anew. I lost my connection to the element of Fire the day I was born—and abandoned. I grew up with white-gloved rules that left little room to explore my passionate, intuitive knowing. When I found Fire's warmth, grace, and safety in the arms of these teachings, I came into my own. Rooted in Five Element wisdom, Maureen's book presents its healing power clearly and creatively for all of us who want to find our best path home."
—**Katherine Metz**,
owner of Feng Shui Storyboard

"*Creating Luminous Spaces* is a wonderful and practical new guide for using ancient Chinese wisdom in our modern lives! Maureen Calamia's caring heart shines through as she shows you, in easy-to-follow steps, how to apply the universal principles of the Five Elements to change your home—and to change your life."
—**Jean Haner**,
author of *Clear Home, Clear Heart:*
Learn to Clear the Energy of People & Places

"Balance within your home promotes balance within you. *Creating Luminous Spaces* will guide you to ancient teachings and show you how to use this knowledge to bring peace and balance to your home, yourself, and your life. It will change the way you think, how you view your surroundings, and how you live."
—**Dr. Eva Selhub**,
author of *Your Brain on Nature*
and *Your Health Destiny*

"With skillful clarity and an open heart, Maureen Calamia offers her gift of light and love. *Creating Luminous Spaces* reminds us how to connect with the sacredness in nature and the world around us to cultivate true joy in our inner and outer environments." **—Anjie Cho**, architect, feng shui expert, and author of *108 Ways to Create Holistic Spaces*

"A refreshing new view of ancient ways to enhance your life. Once you understand that by nature you are nature, the world is your playground. Who doesn't want that?" **—Karen Rauch Carter**, bestselling author of *Move Your Stuff, Change Your Life* and *Make a Shift, Change Your Life*

"I highly recommend this inspirational book! It is a wonderful guide to enhance the Chi energy of your home. In addition to learning simple, elegant, and creative ideas to beautify your sacred spaces, you will gain insights about yourself and your environment. In *Creating Luminous Spaces*, Maureen has given you the power of Mother Nature's tools in your hand." **—RD Chin**, feng shui master and teacher, author of *Feng Shui Revealed*

"The Five Elements is a profound system that can provide a map for life. In *Creating Luminous Spaces*, Maureen K. Calamia utilizes the elements to help you chart your own course by honoring the power of place and the benefits of nature. This book will help you understand yourself better and become keenly aware of your surroundings—plus, it's fun!" **—Dondi Dahlin**, author of the international bestseller, *The Five Elements: Understand Yourself and Enhance Your Relationships with the Wisdom of the World's Oldest Personality Type System*

"A gem of a book! *Creating Luminous Spaces* guides us in 'bringing light into the heart of our homes, and thus our own hearts.' Maureen makes the complicated simple and captures our imagination. If you're curious about elevating the energy of your personal space, this is the book for you!" **—Jan Johnsen**, author of *Heaven Is a Garden* and *The Spirit of Stone*

Creating Luminous Spaces

Use the Five Elements for Balance and Harmony
in Your Home and in Your Life

MAUREEN K. CALAMIA

Conari Press

This edition first published in 2018 by Conari Press,
an imprint of
Red Wheel/Weiser, LLC
With offices at:
65 Parker Street, Suite 7
Newburyport, MA 01950

ISBN: 978-1-57324-733-7
Library of Congress Cataloging-in-Publication Data available upon request.

Cover design by Kathryn Sky-Peck
Interior images by *Fiverr.com*
Interior by Timm Bryson, em em design, LLC.
Typeset in Adobe Garamond Pro

Printed in Canada
MAR
10 9 8 7 6 5 4 3 2 1

*I dedicate this book to my husband Joe
and our children, Allison and Robert.
They are following in our vision to create
their own amazing luminous destinies. Namaste.*

Contents

Introduction

Living in harmony with the Earth brings good fortune.
—Taoist proverb

THE HUMAN-NATURE CONNECTION

The golden rays of the rising sun deepen the shadows of the dark crevices of the volcanic cone that makes up the northwestern part of the Hawaiian island of Maui. I am alone on this beach cove, watching the scene unfold. The only sounds are the ebb and flow of the ocean waves that gently wash over my bare feet and the calls of the morning birds out for their first meal of the day. The bleached Hawaiian sand, so soft, provides a deep pillow of a seat for my body. The cool morning air is filled with the salty scent of the sea and sweet tropical flowers.

It was the first morning of my honeymoon and had such an impact on me that I still use this setting for my meditations. Whenever I go back to that place, my heart rate drops, and my breath syncs up with Mother Earth. I feel calm and supported and nourished. It was a precise moment in my life that I can feel. All of my senses were keen and aware, activated by the sights, sounds, smells, and textures around me. A profound sense of peace and connection to spirit enveloped me. It was sacred.

Nature has that ability—it's a restorative power. Real nature can create calm and balance our body, mind, and spirit. In fact, studies have proven that spending time in nature lowers the heart rate and blood pressure, reduces the production of the stress hormone cortisol, enhances focus, and improves the immune system.

You can harness the light of the universe to achieve higher consciousness, greater joy, and personal power. By tapping into the ancient wisdom of Eastern philosophy and connecting with nature, we can all achieve this.

Wood, fire, earth, metal, and water are not only natural physical materials but also symbols of the different types of energy that make up everything in the universe, from the human personality to thoughts, actions, and words but also seasons and times of day. The Five Elements form an ancient system that is simple and available to all of us. It provides a means to create balance and harmony in our spaces and our lives.

I believe we are poised for the greatest human achievement: a momentous shift in consciousness. I also believe that we create our future, individually and collectively. And we begin this creation with ourselves and our homes. We can start by bringing light into the heart of our homes, and thus our own hearts, and then carrying this light into the world.

WHAT IS A LUMINOUS SPACE?

Luminous: to be full of light, emitting self-generating light, to shine. —Online Etymology Dictionary,

Space: a boundless three-dimensional extent in which objects and events occur. —Merriam-Webster's Dictionary

A luminous space is a place that is restorative and nurturing. It is a place that emits a light from within. It's a place that feels like home and is secure and safe. It is a place you have affection for. It's playful and inspirational as well as a place where you can breathe and expand your vision. A luminous space is full of vitality and life. A luminous space supports you in achieving your highest goals and igniting your personal power.

Pristine nature contains the highest quality of energy available. Some call this light or luminosity. For thousands of years our ancestors intuitively sought out luminous places to create villages and habitats. This land had abundant clean water, good quality soil, and mountains and hills to offer protection from harsh winds and approaching enemies. This land had rich, healthy vegetation and wildlife. It had vitality and all the conditions for a thriving human settlement.

Nature also has a hidden intrinsic power that gives it luminosity. Nature contains a sacred geometry of mathematical ratios, harmonics, and proportion. Patterns are evident in everything from seashells and trees to butterflies and flowers. These patterns are also found in music and light, throughout the human body, and throughout the universe. By studying these patterns, ancient humans found ways to incorporate this wisdom into sacred buildings, music, artwork, and sculpture. Some of these patterns are still incorporated into consciously constructed buildings today.

Luminous spaces engage the senses in a positive experience. They possess natural harmony, are often awe-inspiring, and allow for direct connection with the heavens. They are places where the heartbeat of the Earth is palpable and resonates with our body, mind, and spirit.

My place in Maui is luminous.

For millennia people have talked about the "light" that shines from those experiencing higher consciousness. It is often depicted as the halos above saints, prophets, and deities. Some people can see this light, or aura, emanate from trees, plants, other living things, and even objects. Most of us don't actually see the light, but we can often still sense it or the lack of it.

Artificial spaces can sometimes be luminous. Sacred places such as churches and temples typically have a higher energy and luminosity. However, the standard home or building is usually not a luminous space. Our homes should be places of sanctuary and restoration. They should be places where we can develop and set out to accomplish our hopes and dreams. Our homes should be sacred, and therefore we should treat them with the care they deserve.

Imagine walking in darkness and struggling to find your way. The light, as in religious scripture, can show you the way. It can enlighten you and clarify your direction. Although light is often used as a metaphor, it is also a real thing. You can learn to feel the light in things around you. You can enhance your ability to see the invisible—or rather, what was invisible before.

If you want to increase your energy, your sense of well-being and peace, consider the significance of your home environment. Our homes are a reflection of ourselves and absorb a large part of our identity. They illustrate to us where we are and how we feel about life. They are our refuge from the stress of daily life. Gain a new perspective and identify how you can raise the quality of light in your home to ignite your true nature and personal power with the information and exercises I share here!

How to Use This Book

This book contains practical information, simple exercises, and suggestions to help connect your body, mind, and spirit to nature in a way that you may never have consciously tried before. It is empowering and inspiring.

Each chapter builds upon the previous one. However, if you prefer to jump around, you will still reap the benefits as long as you engage and experiment. Here's an overview of what you can expect in the pages ahead:

Part one (chapters 1–4) is an overview of some amazing ideas about the interconnectedness of our energy, our homes, and nature. You'll be introduced to the Five Elements of feng shui practice and how their energies form an interconnected system. The ideas are meant to prep you on how to connect more deeply to nature as well as open you to a more conscious awareness of the interaction between nature, your home, and your life.

Part two (chapters 5–9) covers each of the Five Elements in depth, with insights on how they come alive in our lives and in our spaces and how to maximize their effects. Each chapter also provides real-life examples of the influence each Element has on us and stories that bring each Element to life. As you get to know the Five Elements, you will start to see how they express themselves in your life and the lives of those you care about. Each chapter will also share exercises on how to connect to the sacred in a way that strengthens our understanding of that Element. As you read through the Element chapters, watch for descriptive words that truly resonate with you and either highlight them or write them down in your journal. If any memories are triggered by the stories, write about them in your journal. This will come in handy for the exercises in part 3.

Part three (chapters 10–11) starts with the What Is Your True Nature? Assessment to identify your True Nature Element—the one Element that represents the most authentic you. Now that you have gotten to know the Five Elements, it is time to dig deeper into your own preferences and motivations to see which one (or two) resonates the most with you. This isn't like zodiac signs where you find out your own symbol and then only read about that in horoscopes; it's about learning what feeds your energy and how all energy moves in an interdependent cycle in tune with nature. This section will help you personalize your home so that it fulfills your desires and needs within that cycle. Part three concludes by showing you how to bring all this information together to create your own luminous spaces inside and out.

The appendix contains a summary of the Five Element information to refer to throughout the book. Chart 1 is a list of words related to the personality traits of each Element. Chart 2 contains a summary of the strengths and weaknesses of each Element. And Chart 3 provides a list of some of the ways that you can connect with each of the Five Elements in your home, your outdoors, and in your life.

My hope is that you treat this book like a longtime friend. Get comfortable with it, make notes in the margins, and turn down pages. Highlight bits that are particularly helpful to you (and remember to do this with words that speak to you in the Elements chapters to get a complete picture in the True Nature Assessment). Journal as you go. You will deepen your awareness of who you really are and what makes you tick. This is sacred stuff.

Notice the signs that appear as you work through these pages: There are synchronicities all around—signs and symbols that can nudge and enlighten you. Pay attention. They are important. Keep track of them! You may want to revisit these as the process continues to unfold.

Dreams are a vehicle for accessing powerful guidance. In dreams, our homes sometimes symbolize our souls and emotional or spiritual development. Dreaming of a childhood home may signify coming to terms with something from our childhood. Dreaming of your current home may be pointing out something that needs attention. For instance, dreaming of a major water leak could show that we need to check our plumbing (both in the home and in our bodies!) or it could represent an overflow of emotions. Dreaming that we are moving into a new, grand home could symbolize that we are stepping into a higher state of consciousness.

There are many things to consider before coming to any conclusion on the message of our dreams. Consider the feeling or emotion you have upon waking from the dream, any other major symbols, your actions and words (if there are any), and other characters in the dream (which often represent aspects of ourselves). Take note of all of these in your journal. The process of writing about your dreams may reveal meanings you might not otherwise take away.

Be open and aware.

As you go through the Element chapters, interact with the Elements in your daily life. Make a game out of it: "What Element came through today when I was hit with this crisis?" or "What Element did I see in my partner when we went out for dinner?" Work with the Elements in your life. They will come alive!

Share with others: See if your partner or children will do the quizzes too and then see how you can help them connect better to nature in their own spaces. Or perhaps bring this book to your book club or start one. Sharing with others enables us to see things from a new perspective, opening up our intuition for both ourselves and those around us.

As you go through the book, be playful and curious. As you do the exercises, experiment and have fun. You'll see how these simple concepts will help you tap into the power of nature to create a more luminous space in your home and experience more balance and harmony in your life.

Please see the Luminous Spaces Community section (p. 219) for additional information on my website.

PART ONE

The Secret of Luminous Spaces

Between every two pine trees there is a door leading to a new way of life.

—John Muir

There is a stand of tall pines on the high school property down the block from my house. Red-tailed hawks and great horned owls like to perch high up on their branches. I've walked among these trees for the past two decades, but the other day, it was different. I approached the trees from a different vantage point and saw something new. It was a portal, or actually it was an opening between two of the pines. The pines stood there resolute, beckoning my attention. As John Muir intuited, I recognized it as an opportunity to enter a door, an opening, with a conscious decision to look at life anew—to feel a perceptible difference in the energy around me and enter a new phase.

In part one of this book, I invite you, too, to enter this beckoning portal. To see your environment, your home, and your life with a new, fresh perspective. I invite you to do this with the conscious intention to make a significant shift in your life.

Learning about feng shui and the Five Elements will change your view of the world. Feng shui is not limited to the arrangement of our homes; it connects us to the vital life force energy of the universe as well as the inner sanctum of our hearts. The Five Elements are but various flavors of this energy and how they interrelate in the real world. You will also be introduced to biophilia and its application, biophilic design, which I found early in my career as essentially a modern take on feng shui.

You will be exposed to some ideas that may or may not seem natural to you. Walk through that opening and see where it takes you!

Chapter 1

Where Do We Start?

Don't you know yet? It's your light that lights the worlds.

—Rumi

An undisturbed natural habitat is in harmony. It has great luminosity. The trees in such a place have created a strong web of connection among their own as well as the other trees in the land. They communicate and have a complicated system of teamwork that we are only starting to understand.

The wildlife is in harmony with the land and each other. The land provides just enough food to support the wildlife and the food chain that has developed over millennia. The ecosystem constantly strives for this balance, course-correcting itself as needed.

When humans entered this habitat millions of years ago, we were part of this balance and part of the ecosystem's ability to course-correct. But as we developed agricultural practices, we outgrew our dependence on the habitat for survival. We were, for the first time, making significant impacts on the land, which allowed us to increase our population. We inevitably upset the inherent balance. Our activities to develop our infrastructure and protect our "ownership" have disturbed the ecosystem and have led to fragmentation and lowered the natural energy of the land.

Although some indigenous tribes and cultures still use ancient ways to determine best placement of structures and ritual and ceremony to honor and respect the land, the only care in modern building practice is toward efficiency and profit. The majority of our homes were built post-WWII, long after industrialization and the development of artificial building materials. These materials have increased efficiency, convenience, and lowered cost, but they do little to enhance the luminosity of our homes.

Many of the conditions of our homes are set: Our homes are on the land it is on—whether it was honored or not. The design and materials it was built with—whether beautiful or used for efficiency's sake, whether handcrafted or machine made—may not be things we can change. So what can we do to make our home a more luminous space?

There are two significant aspects completely within our control:

1. What we put inside our homes physically, mentally, emotionally, and spiritually.
2. What we hold inside of *us*.

OUR HOMES HAVE A POWERFUL IMPACT ON OUR LIVES

Research proves that we are connected to our built environment in unseen ways. Environmental psychology, a branch of psychology established in the mid-twentieth century, studies this connection and the impact of our environments on our cognitive functioning, behavior, and physiology.

Color has a dramatic impact on our emotions and behavior. The color red energizes and even sometimes increases aggression, whereas the color green is calming to most. Blue flooring can sometimes disorient people on a subconscious level as unstable because of its association to water. And dark ceilings make the room feel more closed in, like a cave. Lighting, decor, and many other interior design details can have a huge effect on how we feel in those spaces.

Not only do they influence how we feel, act, and behave in the moment, but when we spend time in them longer term, they will have a great impact on our lives.

The fact that we are so intimately engaged with the spaces in our homes makes the psychology of home even more profound.

THE IMPORTANCE OF NATURE

Since natural environments emit the highest quality of light, incorporating nature into our spaces will increase their luminosity. That is, we should actually bring the outdoors in.

In the 1970s, the psychologist Erich Fromm coined the term "biophilia" to describe humanity's inherent need to connect with all things living. E. O. Wilson, biologist, and Stephen Kellert, professor emeritus at Yale University, coauthored several books on biophilia more recently that have brought this subject to prominence among environmentalists, educators, the health care sector, and even the architectural design industry. The design movement that emerged from this research, biophilic design, is in many ways akin to feng shui. The goal of each discipline is to create a space that will enhance well-being for its inhabitants through a greater connection to nature.

However, how each discipline approaches the end goal couldn't be more different. Biophilic design incorporates a series of well-documented and research-based guidelines for architects and designers. Feng shui provides a philosophy of life that was created from observing the natural world thousands of years ago. One is tangible and finite, and the other is often intangible and intuitive. I like to say biophilic design is the yang, and feng shui is the yin.

For instance, with biophilic design we would use natural materials like wood and brick, the colors of nature, and aspects of nature such as natural light and fresh air. But feng shui speaks to a deeper layer of nature that is communicated through an esoteric language of yin and yang and the five transformations of energy, also known as the Five Elements of Wood, Fire, Earth, Metal, and Water.

Feng shui is rooted in Taoist principles, the ideology that gave rise to the religion of Taoism, and was developed perhaps three to four thousand years ago. One of the two main religions of China, Taoism embodies the belief in the wisdom of nature and its cyclic influences on human affairs. The natural powers of the Cosmic Trinity—the realms of Heaven, Humanity, and Earth—have a corresponding influence on our reality. Their forces interconnect and influence each other and are essential to understanding the movement of energy and patterns of the universe. The fundamental forces of nature include the flow of chi, the theory of yin and yang, and the five natural elements.

In our explorations together, I will incorporate aspects of both feng shui and biophilic design and actually present a merged, synergistic view: Since yin is nothing without its counterpart yang, the two together—the ancient and the modern, the feminine and the masculine—have an important role in creating more beauty, harmony, and balance in our daily lives.

WHAT ARE ENERGY AND CONSCIOUSNESS?

The term *energy* can mean many things. I am referring to it as chi or life force energy in Eastern cultures. Energy is invisible, yet can be more powerful than physical matter. Energy encompasses all matter and what we call empty space.

The term *consciousness* is just as broad and vague. It relates to being awake and aware of our surroundings. But from a traditional viewpoint, this awareness is confined to physical surroundings. In a more profound way, consciousness is being awake and aware to the invisible, spiritual side of existence, as well.

Consciousness is actually the "data" being transmitted by energy. It is easily picked up and felt by intuitive people, yet we all are affected by consciousness, whether we realize it or not.

We tap into the energy and consciousness of an environment all the time. We do it when we notice an office is stuffy or a restaurant feels inviting. We do it with people as well. We can sense that someone is helpful or when someone feels threatening. We developed this intuition over millennia to make snap decisions about a situation, a person, or an environment because it might mean life or death.

Even though a great deal of research has been conducted to understand consciousness, we still know so little. The presence of consciousness now is believed to be with animals, trees, plants, and even water. These "beings" interact with the consciousness in the energy fields around them, and react to events and experiences, just like us. In some fringes of science, consciousness itself is extended to inanimate objects.

You may already recognize a level of consciousness in your home. You may have felt it, as I did, when I first saw my house. There is a subtle welcoming I sense when I come home from a long day away. I have great affection for my home and show my appreciation when I touch the doors and when I hold the wooden rail as I climb the stairs. I will guide you to feel that connection if you don't already have one.

THE DARK AND LIGHT PRINCIPLE

The dark and light principle, also known as yin and yang, deals with complementary opposites. Yin represents the feminine, yielding, quiet, and soft, whereas yang depicts the masculine, active, loud, and hard. These opposites are nothing on their own. They only have meaning relative to one another. For instance, you cannot understand quiet without having loud. You cannot understand light without having experienced darkness.

The yin and yang principle is an amazingly simple yet complex tool that we use every day in our lives. It is in constant play in our homes: When we turn up the light in a room, we look for the balance between pitch dark and blinding light. We adjust the thermostat to get a balance between frigid cold and suffocating heat. When we decorate a room, many of us intuitively strike a balance between yin and yang in the furnishings, window treatments, lighting, flooring, colors. The hardness of wood floors (yang) is wonderfully paired with area rugs (yin). A round dining table complements the hard angles of the dining room. Brightly colored accent pillows work well with a beige sofa.

Striking a comfortable balance between yin and yang is an important part of feeling more connected to nature. Balance is inherent in nature. The ancient sages created a language to explain and mimic nature for our own comfort, security, and well-being.

FIVE NATURAL ELEMENTS

There are fiery sparks of the world soul, of the light of nature, dispersed or sprinkled in and throughout the structure of the great world into all the fruits of the elements everywhere.
—alchemical text

In the Eastern perspective, everything in creation is possible through the interaction of the Five Elements of Wood, Fire, Earth, Metal, and Water. These Elements are more than material. They each embody a different type of energy that together make up a catalyst for change and transformation. Water is descending, Wood is uprising, Fire is ascending, Earth is stable, and Metal is contracting.

The Eastern Elements differ in number from the Western Elements of fire, water, air, and earth. The Western system uses tangible, material, stable categories, while the Eastern system looks at the changes or energy "transforming" from one state to the next. They are more appropriately called the Five Phases or Transformations of Chi, as the material itself is of lesser importance.

Through observation, we learn the wisdom of how nature works and how those Elements support, nourish, drain, control, or dominate to create change. For example, we can see the wonder of a long-awaited rainstorm (Water) on parched land (Fire). Plant life (Wood) springs into life; leaves green and shiny, healthy and strong.

Their color and scent are most vibrant. Or how a lava flow (Fire) consumes everything in its path, including buildings and vegetation (Wood).

It is the chi emanating from each of these five stages that feeds the universe. Everything that exists in the cosmos can be classified by these Elements, and each has inherent qualities that can be used to describe it.

- Wood is the vegetation covering the Earth, providing nourishment to most creatures and beings on the planet. Wood provides shade and oxygen. It provides a sense of vitality of the land. It is springtime and the morning sunrise.

- Fire brings us light and the warmth of the sun as well as the hearth. It is the magma rising up through the Earth, breaking the surface, and spilling over onto the Earth. Fire sweeps through the forest, feeding on the undergrowth and freeing up necessary nutrients for a thriving ecosystem. Fire consumes what is in its path, but it is also the seed process for new creation. The mastery of Fire distinguishes us from all other living creatures. It is excitement and connection. It is summer and noontime.

- Earth is the soil and sand we walk upon and the abundant rocks in the Earth created from millions of years of compression, heat, and erosion. Earth is the horizontal surface, the ground beneath our feet. Earth gives us stability and groundedness. It is early fall and late afternoon.

- Metal is the precious minerals found deep within the Earth. These minerals nourish our water, providing us with necessary nutrients. The ultimate and most coveted of metals is gold, which represents the alchemical process of turning soil into something pure and precious. Metal is also connected to the heavens, stars, and sky. Metal is stardust. It is said to represent the spiritual path from awareness to enlightenment. It is refined and noble. It is late fall and early evening.

- Water quenches thirst, allows for reflection. It can be deep and still like a lake or wild and flowing like a waterfall. It connects the rhythm of our bodies to the ocean. Blood flowing through our veins is like the water flowing on the planet. Where there is water, there is life. The moon is also water energy. It is winter and midnight.

In the following chapters, we explore the concepts of chi, yin and yang, and the Five Elements more deeply.

Chapter 2

Every Space Has Energy and Consciousness

For my ally is the Force, and a powerful ally it is. Life creates it, makes it grow. Its energy surrounds us and binds us. Luminous beings are we, not this crude matter. You must feel the Force around you; here, between you, me, the tree, the rock, everywhere, yes.

—Yoda, *The Empire Strikes Back*

In my workshops, I ask for a volunteer to come up to the front of the room and stand about ten feet away from me. With copper dowsing rods in hand, I approach them slowly until the rods open up. I explain that the rods are an ancient tool used to find underground water and they are also used to measure energy. The rods open when they touch the edge of the volunteer's energy field. You can see the childlike wonder in their eyes, as children are open and curious to the inner, hidden workings of the world.

I then ask the volunteer to think about something really marvelous—something that makes them very happy. I repeat the procedure, but this time, the rods open up sooner—usually a foot or two farther away than they did before. The expansion of energy is palpable. This simple exercise demonstrates more than words ever could how people's thoughts have an impact on their energy.

What the dowsing rods are actually reacting to is the openness of the heart chakra. There are seven main chakras, or energy wheels, within the human body from the base of the spine to the crown of the head. When we think positively, we are actually opening our hearts and embracing the world at large. When we feel fear, anxiety, anger, or depression, our heart chakra closes to the world, and we project these negative emotions. Negative energy weakens our immune system and our physical bodies. Consistent negative thoughts and behavior will lead to illness.

This energy is also known as chi or life force energy in Eastern cultures. *Energy is invisible and subtle yet is often more powerful than any physical matter.* Energy encompasses all matter, nonmatter, and what we call empty space.

Acknowledging that energy pervades the entire universe is essential to the understanding of feng shui, the opposing forces of yin and yang, and the prevalence of the Five Elements. Each living being, rock, building, and piece of artwork contains an energy field, and its energy is in constant interaction with everything else in its surroundings. It isn't simply through our five senses that we engage with our environments. We certainly are impacted by our vision, smells, textures, warmth (or lack of it), as well as sounds and even tastes. However, it is the invisible energy that is often the most powerful and impactful to our experience; mostly because, counterintuitively, since energy is invisible it is easy to dismiss. Christopher Day, architect and author of *Places of the Soul* said, "Most of the time we do not notice our surroundings and then they can work on us with no conscious resistance on our part."

How can we consciously resist what we do not notice? Because we become so used to our surroundings, we are often not consciously engaging with them. They become a backdrop in our lives. Think about this for a moment. Have you ever had someone point something out in your home that you truly didn't notice? Perhaps it was a pile of boxes that have been in the corner of your family room for months that you forgot about, creating stagnant and blocked energy in the room. Or, perhaps the front door is broken, which contributes to poor energy at this vital point connecting us to life force and opportunities. At times, we become numb to our surroundings. It's perfectly human. *But that doesn't mean that their influence in our lives decreases.*

Energy has the potential to make us feel the full range of emotions. Heavy energy can make us feel sick or depressed. Sometimes we can sense the energy of a room after someone had an argument. The first time I felt the energy in a room was a profound experience for me.

It was early in my career when a client brought me in to help with some issues with family and finances. It was my second visit, and I decided that we needed to do a thorough space clearing to lift the vibrations in the home. While we were going through the finished basement, which was being used as a TV room, I noticed that I kept running into cobwebs. I brushed them away from my face, but they kept coming back. This seemed very strange because the client was walking ahead of me, but she didn't show any sign of encountering them.

When we were done, I told her what I had experienced, and she understood immediately. She finally told me the real reason for my visit was to help them get past a traumatic episode in their lives. Her husband had served several years in prison for fraud, and the basement TV room was his refuge throughout the trial. The negative energy was so thick it was palpable!

Conversely, the energy in a sacred place, such as a church, temple, or forest grove, can be uplifting and life-affirming. I felt this energy while at a friend's farm in British Columbia. The land had several groves of old growth trees—Douglas fir, Sitka spruce, bigleaf maple, and red cedar. These places held an uncommon grace and light. Science is only just starting to explore and be receptive to insights into energy and consciousness. We have so much to learn!

Quantum physics proves that we are energy. We are all connected and not separate from the universe. We are electromagnetic beings with an invisible energy field surrounding our physical bodies. We communicate emotion and thought through the vibrations of this energy field. Imagine dropping a pebble into a lake. It creates ripples of water that travel outward. Like the water in the pond, our energy field picks up on the ripples of energy flowing out from those around us. Every life experience we have is influenced by our energy fields and vice versa.

The sun, moon, stars, and planets all radiate energy down through the Earth's atmosphere. This energy is circulated down to the soil and water. It funnels into our buildings through our doors and windows and into our hallways and each room, eventually affecting the energy of all who reside there.

CONSCIOUSNESS

Consciousness is now one of the most studied and yet controversial topics in psychology. But from a philosophical standpoint, consciousness is much more than science can measure. For all time humanity has contemplated the big questions of life: the nature of reality, our existence, the basis of knowledge and reason. From an indigenous and Eastern philosophy perspective, everything in creation has a form of energy and consciousness that interacts and connects with everything else. According to that famous quote attributed to Chief Seattle in a speech to the governor of the Washington Territories, 1854, "Man did not weave the web of life; he is merely a strand in it. Whatever he does to the web, he does to himself."

Energy has a quality—such as positive, bright, and buoyant or negative, dense, and dull—as well as quantity—the expanse of the energy field. According to quantum physics, all matter can be viewed as both particles and waves that vibrate at different frequencies. Consciousness is the information or data, and energy is the medium that transmits the data. I like to think that consciousness floats on the energy particles or waves.

Our personal energy fields are filled with our consciousness. Forward-thinking scientists are furthering the idea that our minds are not contained in our physical brains. Our minds extend out of our physical bodies into our energy field and perhaps even beyond that.

RAISING CONSCIOUSNESS

Consciousness is not just awareness of our surroundings, but rather the level of awareness of our soul. Dr. David R. Hawkins in his book *Power vs. Force*, shares his Map of Consciousness which defines "specific processes of consciousness—emotions, perceptions, or attitudes, worldviews and spiritual beliefs" (*Power vs. Force*, p. 67). The scale ranges from 0 (death) to 1,000 (enlightenment). "All levels above 200 are constructive expressions of power." (p. 75–76)

What I found most hopeful is Dr. Hawkins discussion of our current days: ". . . in the mid-1980's, it (consciousness) suddenly jumped to the hopeful level of 207" (p. 285–286). Dr. Hawkins puts this number in perspective: "Although only 15 percent of the world's population is above the critical consciousness level of 200, the collective power of that 15 percent has the weight to counterbalance the negativity of the remaining 85 percent of the world's people" (p. 282). Hence, we feel the impact when in the company of a highly evolved soul.

I had the good fortune to be in the presence of one such soul when I attended a teaching by His Holiness the 14th Dalai Lama. I have never felt such presence and loving kindness. His spirit, his consciousness, filled the room. I felt that he was a beacon of light sending out plumes of positive energy to all of us in attendance. My physical body was light, and I was filled with joy. He was the most benevolent being I have been in the company of.

Not only do higher-consciousness individuals have a greater impact, but a small percentage of people can have a significant impact on their environment. This is known as the Maharishi Effect. If a small percent of a population organizes their thoughts in a positive (or negative) way, they can make shifts in the consciousness of the larger population.

In fact, there are many organizations that believe in the power of a small group to manifest positive change. We don't *need* a majority of people to make a significant shift in how the environment heals. In 1976 the Transcendental Meditation Organization reported that when just 1 percent of the population was in a meditative state in a community, the crime rate in that same community would drop by as much as 16 percent.

The Global Coherence Initiative, sponsored by the HeartMath Institute, is one such organization that seeks to positively influence the global unconscious. It conducts research into consciousness and organizes projects that aid in raising human consciousness through energetic fields. Their goal is to promote peace and harmony on the earth and among humanity.

Healing energy raises consciousness, not just for humans, but in our spaces. We are all connected—our buildings and everything in them, seen and unseen. We have the tools to enhance the level of consciousness and, therefore, the quantity and quality of light in our lives.

CONSCIOUSNESS OF NATURE

On his way back from the moon as lunar module pilot for the Apollo 14 mission, NASA astronaut Ed Mitchell had an epiphany. But this was not unusual for him. Mitchell was an odd man out among his colleagues in the NASA program from the beginning. To start, he didn't come up through the typical ranks of pilots. He started his career as an engineer and scientist, getting a PhD in science from MIT in 1964. While on this nine-day voyage, Mitchell participated in a number of experiments on telepathy that not even his lunar module colleagues knew about.

But Mitchell's revelation was something more profound. As he viewed the Earth as few had seen it before—filling the view from his window, blue and white and perfect—he felt an immediate oneness. In Mitchell's words:

> Suddenly from behind the rim of the moon, in long, slow-motion moments of immense majesty, there emerges a sparkling blue and white jewel, a light, delicate sky-blue sphere laced with slow swirling veils of white, rising gradually like a small pearl in a thick sea of black mystery. It takes more than a moment to fully realize this is Earth—home. . . . On the return trip home, gazing through 240,000 miles of space toward the stars and the planet from which I had come, I suddenly experienced the universe as intelligent, loving, and harmonious.

Mitchell was so moved by his experience that within two years he founded the Institute of Noetic Sciences (IONS). *Noetic* comes from the Greek word *nous*, which means "intuitive mind." This nonprofit organization, stronger than ever, primarily sponsors and participates in primary research into consciousness and healing with the belief that consciousness is essential to a paradigm shift that will lead to a more sustainable world. When we raise our consciousness to new levels, we will have no other choice then to become stewards of this Earth.

Over the last few decades, Dr. Masaru Emoto, author of *Messages in Water*, has conducted groundbreaking studies into the crystalline properties of water. What he found was almost unbelievable: water crystal formation responds to the positive or negative energies in the surrounding environment. When there is benevolent energy directed toward the water, it forms beautiful, geometric crystals. When negative energy is directed toward the water, the crystals that do form are deformed and hideous.

Dr. Emoto makes the connection between our physical bodies and the properties of water. The human body is roughly 70 percent water. So if water responds to energy, be it positive or negative, our bodies surely do as well. His experiments are physical proof on how our bodies respond to the energies of our environments. It is truly amazing work.

In light of this concept, the Taoist proverb "Living in harmony with the Earth brings good fortune" makes complete sense. Indigenous cultures all over the world have worshipped the Earth and her bounty, even sacrificing to the gods of the land and sky so that their tribes would be bestowed with good crops and prosper. Positive attention and care reap positive impact.

In his *New York Times* best seller, *The Hidden Life of Trees*, Peter Wohlleben discusses the complex lives of trees. Trees support each other by sharing nutrients and water and communicate alerts about infestation so their neighbors can defend themselves. They have the ability to intelligently respond to changes in the environment, recalling what to do in stressful periods months or even years later. They have some different form of intelligence and consciousness that we weren't aware of until recently.

If trees and plants have consciousness and water has consciousness, what about a rock?

If we share this interrelationship with vegetation, then what about the habitat in which that vegetation survives? It makes complete sense that, overall, our thoughts, our emotions, and our intentions will have an impact on the land as well.

These examples show the powerful feedback loop that exists: We interact and affect the land and the land interacts and affects us. Land that is blessed emanates a strong, positive energy that, if we could see it, would be a rainbow of translucent, bright full-spectrum light—just like some utopian land. When we see such a place, we identify with its goodness, its richness, and its benevolence. It is intuitive, sometimes not rational, yet registers with a primordial part of our brains. On the other hand, we also quickly identify with places that have been damaged or neglected. These places project a dull, dark aura we recognize as draining or threatening. Whether traumatized by conflict, war, excavation, or wasteful farming and building practices, the entire habitat will suffer, move, or die away.

The Earth also emits energy fields from the electromagnetic grid that encircles it, as well as underground streams, open cavities, and various forms of rock strata. The energy is generally benign, but when there is trauma to the Earth or other negative forces, these fields can become harmful to human life. This is called geopathic stress, and research has been done that links this stress to human illness and degradation of the land.

By isolating ourselves within the confines of buildings in our modern cultures we are also shutting ourselves off from even benevolent nature. This extreme divergence has accelerated over the last century, and many believe we are at a tipping point. In our quest for the "advancement" of civilization we have ignored the roots that have kept us connected to the positive energy of the natural world. Being of nature ourselves, we are feeling the impact of this shift. We are only now coming to understand the consequences on our body, mind, and spirit.

In the last decade, there has been a real movement to foster a greater connection to nature: the "New Nature Movement" championed by author Richard Louv in his best-selling books, *The Last Child in the Woods* and *The Nature Principle*. Louv talks about this worldwide and has founded the nonprofit Children & Nature Network, whose mission is to connect children and families to nature. Louv was inspired by research on the benefits of nature to combat a global rise in stress-related illness, depression, and anxiety. The basic premise is that our own health is connected to the health of the Earth, but since the Industrial Revolution, we are, for the first time in our evolution, spending more of our time inside than outside. We spend roughly 90 percent of our days in buildings. There is an urgent need to reestablish our connection to nature both in the natural world and in our man-made spaces.

BETWEEN HEAVEN AND EARTH

According to Chinese cosmology, as with most other religious traditions, in the beginning there was a void, and out of this void sprang forth the duality of feminine and masculine, or yin and yang. These are two opposing but complementary forces. Yang represents Heaven and yin represents Earth. They are both forms of chi or life force energy.

Yin and yang are dependent upon one another. Both are required for the universe to exist. We cannot know one without the other. How would we know light if we did not know dark? An object is neither yin nor yang. It is only in relationship to another object that we can discern the complementary qualities. For instance, a wood floor is yang (hard) when compared to a carpeted floor (soft). But when compared to a stone floor (hard), the wood floor is more yin (soft).

Neither yin nor yang is bad or good. Those judgments do not apply to these sacred concepts. What is considered bad or inauspicious is when yin and yang are completely out of balance. In the current state of the world, we are going through an extremely yang phase. We are unbalanced as a global society. We have gone to the extremes of the masculine, yang energy as witnessed by cultural obsessions with activity and achievement, rather than equally valuing quiet reflection and stillness. However, the emergence of ancient and indigenous earth teachings (the feminine yin energies) are shifting us back into balance. The rise of Eastern practices of meditation and yoga in the West is a positive movement toward this balance. With the right amount of enlightened souls approaching a tipping point, their thoughts and actions can raise the world's consciousness to a new state. And change can happen very quickly.

The yin-yang symbol is packed with information. It shows the flow of chi transitioning from one state to the other. It can be overlaid onto any life cycle. Within the calendar, it demonstrates the energy of the seasons. Yang (the masculine) peaks at the summer solstice (the peak of the sun). The seed of yin begins to grow immediately after and flourish until the winter solstice where yin peaks. At this point, yin (the feminine) is now giving way to the yang again. Yin and yang are also on display in the cycle of the day and life spans of all living beings. Both yin and yang each contain a seed of the opposing energy to allow for transitions to occur. This ensures the continuance of cycles of change.

The resonance of yin and yang in relationship between humanity and nature is of supreme importance. The energy of the Heavens (yang) is said to flow down to the Earth (yin), which collects and sends it back up, forming all of life, including humanity. A Cosmic Trinity is thus formed: Heaven, Humanity, and Earth. This Trinity, showing the energetic connection between the Divine, Humanity, and Nature, appears symbolically in many world religions: in Christianity as the Father, the Son, and the Holy Spirit; in Hinduism as Brahma, Vishnu, and Shiva; for the Egyptians as Osiris, Isis, and Horus.

———————— Heaven

———————— Humanity

———————— Earth

In this system of energy, it is our duty to remain respectful of what gives us life and to maintain integrity with all we create and destroy. The Chinese believe that if you harness your environment in such a way, it is the path to good fortune, which translates to a thriving life:

- If you improve the energy of your home, you will impact your outlook and actions.
- If you improve your outlook and actions, you will improve your destiny.
- If you improve your destiny, you will improve your chances for success and attract your greatest dreams.

In this way, we are "in the flow" of life; we harness the power of balance and harmony. We strengthen our energetic immune system and achieve greater health and well-being. We strengthen our inner power.

IS MY HOME CONSCIOUS?

Our homes are conscious, but not in the traditional sense. At some level, our homes react to our actions and behavior. If we neglect our homes by failing to perform routine maintenance, they will take on a state of neglect. They will feel chaotic and will not seem like sanctuaries and places of rest. On the other hand, if we give our home the attention it needs, its energy will lift to provide a caring shelter. It will reflect the positive, peaceful energy back to you.

As I mentioned earlier, quantum physics proves that everything is alive and animated. The cells of everything around us are vibrating at vast speeds. Science is coming to terms with the fact that nature is sentient—and more so than we would have ever guessed. It makes decisions, feels pain, and has empathy. It may not have the same consciousness as we do, but nevertheless, as with trees and water, there is energy and consciousness at some level.

As this universal energy merges with the energetic vibrations of everything in our homes, it creates energetic patterns that impact our physical bodies and thoughts and influence our emotions and behavior. We, in turn, also transmit energy to our environments, attracting certain energetic patterns into our lives. We attract what we send out. If we live in a state of lower consciousness, we can attract frustration, anger, illness, depression, as well as challenging relationship, work, and life circumstances. If we raise our consciousness, we will attract those lower-level experiences less and less, and when we do, we will have a more positive response to them. We will see them as vehicles for our personal growth.

When we understand this connection between our environments and our well-being, we can make positive shifts in our homes that will impact our energetic patterns and create more luminous spaces, both within and without. Increasing the luminosity of our home will expand our inner light, raise our consciousness, and activate our true, authentic power.

The level of consciousness of our environments has an impact on our own consciousness, and that energy radiates out to others in a never-ending feedback loop. The scale doesn't need to be huge to have an impact. As the Maharishi Effect shows, a small percentage can make all the difference. This awareness of how we are continually interacting with our environments and those around us can help us make a positive difference.

Any philosopher or spiritual guru will tell you that you cannot change anyone but yourself. Self-awareness, self-inquiry, and self-knowledge are the key to spiritual growth. Once you acknowledge your participation in any situation or relationship, that awareness can provide you with the keys to new perception that may just create the shifts and change you are looking for in your life.

CONNECTING WITH THE
CONSCIOUSNESS OF YOUR HOME

Have you named your car? Lots of people do. I purchased a new car a few years ago and named it immediately: Indiana Jones! Yes,

I wanted to inspire the feeling of adventure, courage, and discovery in my new vehicle so it would reflect back my desires for these qualities in my life. Indy would bring me on new beginnings and adventures, across the borders and down the proverbial paths to my future. Once named, I felt affection for her (yes, her!). I talk to her and stroke her dashboard often and give thanks for her loyal and dependable service.

According to psychologists, this is called anthropomorphism, the act of assigning human characteristics or behavior to an animal or object. It is mostly associated with animistic and shamanic traditions; however, in Western society we sometimes associate spirit with inanimate objects as well.

Now that you understand how your home can have consciousness, do you feel more connected to it? How about a name? There is a tendency to name grand estates and mansions. The Breakers, a Vanderbilt mansion in Newport, Rhode Island, is named for the fantastic surf at the base of the cliff that the home resides on. Fallingwater, one of Frank Lloyd Wright's architectural gems, is named for the waterfall that it sits atop. What name would you give your home?

THE HEART OF THE HOME

Our homes absorb energy over time. They absorb the energy of the features of the land they are on as well as all the earth energies, whether positive or negative. They absorb the thoughts and actions and life situations of all of the occupants of the home. This energy is retained within the structure until ritually released. These space clearing ceremonies are often performed with incense, sound, and prayer.

The "heart" of the home is where all of this energy is connected, like a matrix. Once we connect to the heart, we can start the space clearing process.

- First, expand your energy field. Sense how your immediate energy field swells when you exhale. Breathe in and out, and with each breath gently expand your field to fill your entire home. What feels like the heart of your home? Where do you gravitate to? It might be the physical center of your home or it might be a favorite spot where everyone naturally gathers. It might be a fireplace or where your reading chair is located.
- If you are having difficulty finding the heart of your home, use the formal front entrance. The front door represents the Mouth of Chi or primary energy gateway to your home. Besides the heart, it is a space of extreme importance to acknowledge.
- Second, go to the location of the heart. If you are using the front door, open it. Stand in that space or facing the outside of the front door. Rub your hands together quickly a few times to activate your palms, and then hold them a few inches from the nearest wall or door. You may feel a tingly or warm sensation in your palms. You may sway a little forward then backward. I call this "dancing" with the energy. You are feeling the connection.
- Once you establish connection, see what comes up. Perhaps you'll get a message from your home, what it needs, what it desires, how it feels. This might show up as a feeling you get somewhere in your body. It might be in the form of an image or a sound. You might see in your mind's eye a blue door instead of a white one. Your door might be saying that it wants to be painted red. Or maybe a bird chirps close to you on the porch, which could be a sign of communication and welcome from your home. We are all unique beings and have different strengths of intuitive knowing. There are no right or wrong answers here. Don't discard your ability to do this or second-guess your thoughts.

I once heard the sound of laughter when I did this exercise for a client. The message for my client was to be more lighthearted and perhaps have a party! In another consultation, I received an image of red. When I asked my client about it, she said that she had been contemplating repainting one wall in her office a beautiful shade of red. Well, the house certainly responded with a big yes!

RELEASING ENERGY

Once you have established a connection with your home, you can perform a space clearing ritual to release any unwanted negative energy. This ritual will be conducted in the heart of your home or at the front entrance.

I like to begin by lighting a candle on a simple temporary altar where I've placed flowers, a statue of a deity (I use a Buddha), and perhaps a quartz crystal (which helps expand the energy). State your intentions to clear the home of any negative energy that has accumulated over the years. Next, ask for assistance from the divine source of energy—be it God, Jesus, Buddha, Muhammad, nature spirits, your higher self, your spirit guides, or all of the above. This is the invocation. Using a tool of your choice—incense, smudge stick, bells, or something else—move around your home in a clockwise fashion, taking care to spread the smoke or sound into each corner and closet. Visualize that you are shaking up and removing the negative energy that has settled over the years. (Smudging is a popular clearing technique from Native American traditions using smoke from a stick of sage, a strong incense.)

Go into each room of the house and on each floor, including the basement and garage. When you are done, visualize that this energy is being sucked out of your home through any windows, doors, chimney, and cracks. Your home is now free of this energy. But you are not done. Please be sure to also give your house a blessing.

BLESSING CEREMONY

Blessings can be very elaborate or very simple. Here is a simple version you can use and tailor to make it personal.

Stand at the heart of your home or at the front door. Say a heartfelt prayer of your choice and ask that divine golden white light fill every space, every corner, every closet in your home.

Imagine your intentions and goals for this space as you practice this visualization. For instance, you may ask for help in attracting wonderful opportunities in your career, for continued health for you and your family, and/or to attract a healthy romantic relationship. Set this intention in your heart. Finally, give thanks for the assistance you are receiving here from the higher realms. You can give an offering of flowers, fruit, or incense on your altar. Close the ceremony by blowing out the candle.

CREATING A PERMANENT ALTAR

Altars are wonderful reminders of the sacred in our daily lives. Pick a location that is good for you. Many people keep their altar in their bedrooms. Some place it in their family room or foyer.

All you need is a small tabletop to rest a few items that feel sacred to you. I always place an icon of a deity, such as a Buddha or a Jesus, and a candle. I love to add items from nature, such as a vase with fresh flowers, a rock or crystal, a shell or a pinecone. You can add photographs of loved ones. Embellish the altar as much or as little as you want. Be sure to acknowledge and tend to your altar often. Clear out and replace the flowers. Discard any used candles. Change up the items or photographs. Light the candles and say a prayer before it often. Encourage others to use the altar for their prayers and intentions, as well. Frequent use and mindfulness of this space expands the power of the altar and enhances your feelings of well-being as well as raises the light of your home.

Chapter 3

Our Homes Mirror Our Lives

The house is indeed a mirror of the self if we can learn to interpret what we see, comprehend what it means, and act on what it seeks to communicate.

—Clare Cooper Marcus, *House as a Mirror of Self: Exploring the Deeper Meaning of Home*

At the very core of connection, our homes fill a basic psychological need for shelter and safety. But they should do a lot more than that. They should provide connection with others and a sense of belonging, space for rest and replenishment. If your home does not satisfy these needs, it will create disharmony in your life.

Beyond basic needs, our homes hold powerful symbolic and psychological significance in our lives.

As culture and society have shifted the emphasis and meaning of the role of family and work in our lives, the role of our homes has evolved, too. These changes can be categorized in three main ways: away from familial connections, as a canvas for creative self-expression, and as a respite from today's stressors.

FAMILIAL CONNECTIONS

Not that long ago our homes were filled with extended families. If extended family members were not living in the same house, they were often next door or no more than a block away in the same community. Although there were advantages and disadvantages to this, our families were generally a great source of support and assistance.

I have had the advantage of living close enough to my mother and mother-in-law, who both helped care for my children when I went back to work. In fact, we eventually purchased a house that had a separate apartment for my mother-in-law, and she has been a huge support for me over the twenty-plus years she has lived with us. Now we are helping her as she ages. But most people I know live separate from their extended family and it is not uncommon for families to live thousands of miles apart.

Fewer people in the home usually means less space is required; however, the prevailing trends reveal the opposite. The new average home has nearly double the square footage per person since the 1970s. All this extra space can lead to feelings of isolation as the few family members in the home are dispersed throughout the greater square footage.

Other trends have further increased feelings of isolation. The focus on the backyard as an outdoor "room" reduces the opportunity to socialize with neighbors and passersby on the front porch. Research has shown that vaulted ceilings in newer homes can lead to feelings of formality rather than intimacy, perhaps due to the echoing of our voices. There is a proliferation of rooms that exist for single functions such as studies, craft rooms, home offices, exercise rooms, media rooms, and so on. One of my clients even had a gift-wrapping room!

In my work, I often see couples living in homes large enough for a family of six or eight. There are so many rooms they clearly don't need. How often they use these rooms is only a guess. All these extra spaces contribute to physical and emotional separation. In addition, we often fill our spaces with more material things.

With fewer and fewer members per household, and often thousands of miles between, our homes themselves play a more vital role in providing us with a sense of connection—if not a human connection, then one to the vitality of the natural world.

HOME FOR CREATIVE SELF-EXPRESSION

Most of us take pride in our homes. They are a mirror of ourselves. We often identify with them, with the decor and the artwork we hang on the walls. Our homes can be an authentic or inauthentic expression of who we are. They sometimes serve as a facade showing the face we want others to see. This is why interior decorating is such a huge market; volumes of products, trends, design services, television shows, books, and websites all want to tell us how we can create the home of our dreams. Taking time to infuse your home with your personality can be a source of great creativity and satisfaction, but if we are designing our homes based on prevailing trends and what is available at HomeGoods, we are missing the point.

HOME AS A SANCTUARY

Few would argue that our lives are moving at a faster pace. Technology, which once was touted to reduce our workloads, has only increased our capacity and access 24/7. Stress from digital devices, crowding, urban noise, and even suburban noise from power tools like lawn mowers and leaf blowers continues to grow.

On top of workplace, social, and familial stress, our lives are compounded by environmental stress such as indoor toxic pollutants and electromagnetic fields. Our home should be our place of sanctuary, but unfortunately, for many it is not. This contributes to illness, depression, and/or aggression.

One sure way to improve our home environment is to incorporate aspects of nature. Nature stimulates the parasympathetic or relaxation response, opposed to the fight-or-flight response that we are so used to activating day to day. Incorporating natural elements in our homes can restore the intimate connection to nature that we lack.

For many of us, our lives have become hectic, disconnected, lonely, and often lacking in authenticity. Our homes are a reflection of that lifestyle. We may fill our homes with "stuff" that is actually "clutter" in the attempt to fill a void in our lives both emotional and deeply spiritual. We rationally know that happiness, joy, and contentment cannot be bought, yet we behave in a contradictory fashion. We shop in big-box stores and buy products made with synthetic material filled with thousands of chemicals. We live in a disposable culture and become obsessed with short-lived trends rather than engaging with meaningful and authentic expression.

And then we wonder why everything just doesn't work. We don't feel "at home." We don't feel connected. We don't feel joy.

Clients often tell me that their house doesn't feel like *home*. That is a very sad state indeed. If you agree, then perhaps we can turn that around together. And even if you feel that your home is cozy and warm and represents the authentic you already, we can certainly add some enhancements by fine-tuning your connections.

"BREATHING" THEM IN

Although I love science, I wish scientists put more emphasis into holism than reductionism. Reductionist theory works on the assumption that complex systems can be pared down to simpler, basic parts. Holist theory operates on the idea that the whole is greater than the sum of its parts. Holist theory is paramount when studying the impact of nature on human behavior.

When psychologists study behavior as it relates to, say, a group of trees in an urban space, they try to pinpoint what it actually *is* about the trees that improve behavior: is it the color green, the shade they create, the shapes of the leaves? Yet we intuitively know that it isn't any *one* of those variables. It is the sum of those variables—the group of trees in their entirety—that has a positive impact on how we feel.

Just as architect Christopher Day said, we don't just look at our environments, we *breathe them in*. We take in entire scenes: the quality of sunlight, shadow, variety of colors and textures, varying heights and objects in relationship to one another, the background and foreground. And although our visual sense is our predominant sense, the other four senses and even our sixth sense are taking in data and assimilating and interpreting it, too. This is Survival 101 and is still very much a part of how we experience spaces.

Also, the idea of breathing spaces in brings up another notion. When we breathe spaces in, they become part of us and who we are. Have you ever felt you wanted to quickly leave a place you found off-putting—such as somewhere filled with clutter or a home with stale air? We don't want to accept these influences into our energy field. We may even partially hold our breath. I can think back to such a place I visited not long ago, and I can still feel my body recoiling—in a physical and energetic way—from the energy of that place. I even did a shrug and shake when I left, just like my dog does when she comes in after a rainstorm.

On the other hand, we linger in places that feel wonderful. We take deep breaths and absorb all that we can with all of our senses. We gladly accept that wonderful energy into our bodies and energy fields. We make a space for them. They do not just reside in our minds. They reside in our hearts and souls. Think of a warm family room with a fire and a cozy reading chair or a wonderful sunlight-filled room with lots of plants. My place in Maui is forever a part of me.

PSYCHOLOGY OF HOME

Think of all the homes you've lived in. For some of us, there has only been one. Others of us have lived in several homes for various periods of time. Those homes, like it or not, are *part* of us. Locations, neighborhoods, shapes and colors, conditions, objects, furnishings, nooks and crannies, sounds, smells, and the land—it's all been inhaled into our energetic bodies.

Consider your current home. Perhaps flashes of feelings and emotion rise up. Perhaps this home reminds you of one from your past. According to author and professor of architecture Clare Cooper Marcus, if our childhood home was a safe haven, we often try to recreate aspects of that home in our subsequent residences. Is there something about your home now that reminds you of your childhood?

All the walls of the common rooms in my childhood home were boring painter's beige. The color was noncommittal, lacking self-expression, and bland, but no one could find fault with a beige room. I came to the realization that I carried a fear of color with me into my adult homes.

When we first moved into my current house, it was freshly painted—you guessed it—painter's beige. It felt safe. After a few years of living with those walls, I somehow got inspired to try some color in my pantry. I figured the pantry was a safe room to test, and I went with a bright blue and bright yellow (bold colors!). However, it looked so good it started a painting craze, and I redid one room at a time, bringing life and vitality to all of our common rooms.

The master bedroom was one space that still felt drab to us even with all the sunlight it got. We continued to wake up to painter's beige for a long time, not able to agree on what color we wanted. Then, a vision came to me to use a dark blue. Given the abundant sunlight, this dramatic hue actually feels right. Depending on the exterior light, the walls change from gunmetal to a medium blue. The walls feel rich and cozy. The color is perfect for our sleep haven and, as you'll see later, complements my Wood.

TAKE A MINUTE TO REFLECT ON YOUR HOME

Remember that your home has its own energy and a level of consciousness. Your home is animated. It has life. It breathes in a way; it has sensory perception (although different from ours).

Find a quiet space where you won't be interrupted. Take out some paper and markers or a pen. I'd like for you to reflect on some questions and take your time. Don't think too deeply about the questions or your initial responses. Try to let your intuitive voice shine through. Just go with the flow. You may want to draw your responses, journal, or both—it's your choice. You might be surprised by what comes up. Your responses will come in handy later.

Go with the questions that seem to lead you places. Skip the ones that don't. Breathe in the energy of your home. Hear the silence, feel the invisible. . . .

- What were the circumstances around finding this home? Who selected it and why?
- What was your first gut reaction to this home? Did you like it immediately or not? Why?
- If your home had a personality, what would it be like?
- Does it feel alive? Why?
- What brings you joy in your home? What drains you?
- Do you feel affection and playfulness in your home? What makes you feel this way?
- What is your favorite place to sit and why?
- What says "you" in your home? What objects are an expression of your authentic personality?
- Is there a common theme to the artwork you have? What does it say about you and what you value?
- Is there a common theme to the objects you have? What do they say about what you value?
- What does the reflection of your home say about you?
- What do the color choices say about you?

- What is the land like? What are the features? What is the energy like?
- What do you need your home to be that it isn't now?
- Is there anything about your home that reminds you of your childhood home?
- Is there a common theme to your responses? Any other insights?

Switch gears for a bit and imagine that *you* are the home. It takes a bit of imagination to make this role reversal, but have fun and imagine. First, take a deep breath and close your eyes. Imagine that with each breath your energy field expands. It eventually fills the room you are in. Several breaths later, your energy field encompasses the entire home, perhaps your entire property, including trees, gardens, and other landscaping.

As you go through the next series of questions, let any thoughts or ideas bubble up to the surface of your consciousness and flow out. Do not filter. You might be surprised as you review your thoughts after you are done.

- Who are you? Do you have a name?
- How do you feel about me/us living here?
- Do you feel loved?
- Are you missing anything?
- Do you feel "whole"?
- What about the trees? Gardens? Wildlife? How do they feel?
- Is there something that you want me to know?

Do not let your rational mind interpret what you write or draw. Write your responses quickly.

Now consider your responses. What does your home say about your life and how you feel about it?

Keep this journal entry at hand as you continue reading this book. Add any thoughts to it as you go. You might connect with this information on a different level as you work through later exercises.

DYNAMIC CONNECTION TO OUR SPACES

Sometime during my feng shui training I came across the notion that we didn't so much select our homes, but that our homes *selected us*. I had never heard that before nor even considered that as a possibility, yet it resonated with me deeply.

A friend recently told me about buying her current home many years ago. She and her husband found a community they wanted to live in. It had a great school district, reasonable taxes, and beautiful homes. When they contacted their real estate agent, she said there were no homes on the market in that town that fit their needs but she did know of a couple that might be looking to relocate soon. After meeting my friend and her husband, this couple decided to sell their home to them. The couple said they were reminded of themselves as a young couple thirty years earlier. Everything with the sale went smoothly, and my friend and her husband found themselves in the house of their dreams.

Twenty-plus years ago we were looking for a house. We wanted to live in a better neighborhood with better schools, more space for our family, *and* have a ready-made first floor apartment for my mother-in-law. It was a tall order to fill on our smallish budget.

But we found what we needed. In fact, it was the first house we saw. And while touring the home with the agent, I quietly whispered to my husband that I *had* to have this house! It was like I was meeting an old lover, an old friend. I was heartsick when we left. The house had *soul*. There was richness in the wood floors throughout and moldings in each room. You could tell that the house had been looked after with care. There were many other signs of attention to detail, too many to list here. But beyond what I could see with my eyes, I sensed belonging and love that I cannot put into words. It just felt like a home for us.

The house was perfect. It hit all of our strict criteria and was being offered at a reasonable price, but even more than that, it called to me as a loving friend and embraced my family. And still does.

What was going on with this connection between me and the house? It was about energy and consciousness and the law of attraction. First, let's look at who built this house—not just who commissioned it to be built, but who actually constructed it, too!

The couple who purchased the land had an architect draw up the plans based on their needs. With plans in hand, the husband and his good friend labored for nearly two years, building everything including the intricate plumbing and built-in cabinetry and radiator covers.

Let's look at the bones of the house. Many of the materials used for my house were salvaged from other buildings being torn down in Brooklyn. The cast-iron radiators, brass plumbing, and even the rafters (double the size necessary) were obtained from a Brooklyn monastery dismantled in the 1950s. Those rafters carry a sense of sacredness and love.

Now let's think about the lives of the people that spent time here and the patterns of energy and consciousness they created. The ground floor apartment was refuge for several extended family members needing a place to stay over the years. This was a caring, loving family who helped those in need.

Only last year, a young woman named Aimee approached my house from the street. I noticed her standing there while I was working on my computer. I called to her at the door and found that her grandfather had been the one to lovingly build this house. As a child, Aimee had stayed with her grandparents for many a summer and visited often over the years. The depth of her emotion while walking through the house was heartwarming, as she was delighted to see how we cared for it. The house holds a deep place in her heart.

In talking with Aimee, we were amazed at the synchronicities in our lives. She and her husband Noel practice acupuncture, and my daughter Allison was attending acupuncture school. We marveled at the fact that even I, as a feng shui practitioner, use the same fundamental Chinese principles in my work. And finally, Noel attended college in the Adirondacks in upstate New York and ran on the cross-country team, same as my son Bobby!

As she was leaving, Aimee and I exchanged business cards even though I wasn't sure we would be connecting ever again, but as fate had it, she had an interest in feng shui. She later became a student in my feng shui certification program. It is so gratifying to have Aimee and her family in my life. Although our energies have merged on the physical plane, they've also merged in the spiritual realm. There is a sense of completeness in our relationship, of interconnectedness.

Whether we realize it or not, there is always a powerful attraction and merging of like energies, for bad or good. For us, we connected to a house that has brought us much joy and happiness in our lives, and we attracted lots of positive chi in the form of people as well as opportunity.

But not everyone has the kind of experience I've had. Many people find connections of the negative kind. Just like us, some buildings have old "souls," and some are new; some are positive, and others are negative. The main contributing factors to the quality of energy are the land, the building materials, and workmanship; the people who have occupied the home; and events that have taken place over the years. If the land was dishonored in the past, it may be still holding on to that negative energy. Such influences come in the form or human tragedy, battles, toxic dumping, and even modern construction practices that do not honor the land in ceremony prior to construction.

Due to the massive exodus to the suburbs post-WWII, we find the majority of American houses are "young souls" and have some energy issues. The land was not honored when many of these homes were built; they were often put up quickly, with cheap material and little care from the builders or workers. Many of these homes, even to this day, still retain the effects of that amassed negative energy.

The people inhabiting these homes may have contributed to the low-energy pattern over the years or turned the energy around. It depends on their life events and care for their surroundings.

Some of us that are sensitive to energy can actually feel the negative energy in a home as a general body response (like the feel of those cobwebs), sounds, smells and even visual cues. These people get a gut feeling or a sense of dread when they enter such a space. Some see dark energy hovering around a space or smell a dank, unpleasant odor. They are tapping into the accumulated energy of the home, which can be released and refreshed with an energy space clearing and blessing ceremony.

YIN-YANG: MORE ON THE LIGHT AND DARK PRINCIPLE

In our Western minds, when we think about "balance," we tend to consider it an unachievable state that only the supreme yogis can attain. But balance is a transitory state. There is no "here" or "there" when we are in balance. We are in fleeting moments of stasis and harmony.

What our real goal should be is to live somewhere in the middle of that realm of balance, oscillating, just as atoms do, with various micro movements *around* balance. The closer we are to that middle, in our everyday lives, the greater our joy and well-being. To live somewhere close to that "golden mean" on a daily, even hourly basis means that we have a smaller range of emotions and our vibrational pattern is fairly calm. We have more clarity and light within us.

Balance

When we react to every situation in our lives moment to moment, we are going from one extreme to the other, and that creates frenetic vibrations within us and blocks in our chi.

Picture this: You go to your morning yoga class and feel calm and peaceful. But when you leave the parking lot, someone cuts you off and you flip them the bird.

Some people's emotions and vibrational patterns swing wildly. Their set point is either or both extremes. They seem to thrive on drama or might be in a self-defeating pattern from years of trauma and abuse. They create circumstances that give them the odd satisfaction of being the victim. "See," they say, "it happened to me again!" At the extreme, a manic-depressive or bipolar personality frequently experiences the extremes of yin (stagnation/depression) and yang (chaotic/anxious) and is less often able to settle in that middle state. In fact, many people rarely get to dwell in that middle realm of balance for long.

The law of attraction teaches us that thoughts, words, and actions draw success or its lack into our lives. The Eastern cultures believe that being in harmony means that you are in accord with the cosmos, with the natural flow of energy. Things go smoothly when in harmony. Harmony and balance are reflected in the vibrational patterns within the physical, mental, emotional, and spiritual bodies. If you are in a state of balance, everything you do will come from that place of balance. And if you are in a state of imbalance, everything you do will come from that imbalance: your thoughts, your words, and your actions. Your choices will be impacted by your vibrations. Vibrations reflect the overall state of consciousness of the individual.

BALANCE IN THE HOME

I think we've all had experiences like when we are house-hunting and get an immediate sense that a place isn't right. Sometimes I knew immediately when pulling up to a house if I wanted to go inside or not. It wasn't just the curb appeal or lack thereof; there was a palpable feeling that something was wrong.

It's hard to put a finger on that impulse. In my attempt to wrap my arms around this energy—be it positive or negative—I created a scale I call the Luminosity Scale of 1–100, with 1 being the lowest possible energy/consciousness and 100 being the highest. It is essentially a scale measuring yin and yang with yang being the light principle and yin being the dark principle.

Although somewhat intuitive, the scale has helped me evaluate the relative energy of spaces before and after consultations, confirming for me what I am feeling as well as providing an understanding of the general quality of objects or spaces rated high on the scale versus low on the scale.

SIDE NOTE: There is an alternative dimension to yin and yang in Eastern philosophy beyond the complementary forces we've already considered that is less frequently discussed. In this context, yin represents death and decay, whereas yang represents life and vitality. Again, neither yin nor yang is judged as bad or good, as both conditions are required for the cycle of life. But in terms of human health and well-being, the higher the yang chi, the better. We also experience this when evaluating geopathic stress (negative earth energy). Lines designated as negative are yin—good for decay of organic material—and positive lines are yang—which promote growth and health.

MEASURING THE QUALITY OF ENERGY

Some people may use kinesiology for this practice, but I am more comfortable with using dowsing rods or a pendulum and the Luminosity Scale.

I let a pendulum swing (or use one dowsing rod) to the scale on the outer ring to find the ten-point reading (for instance 51-60)

Luminosity Scale

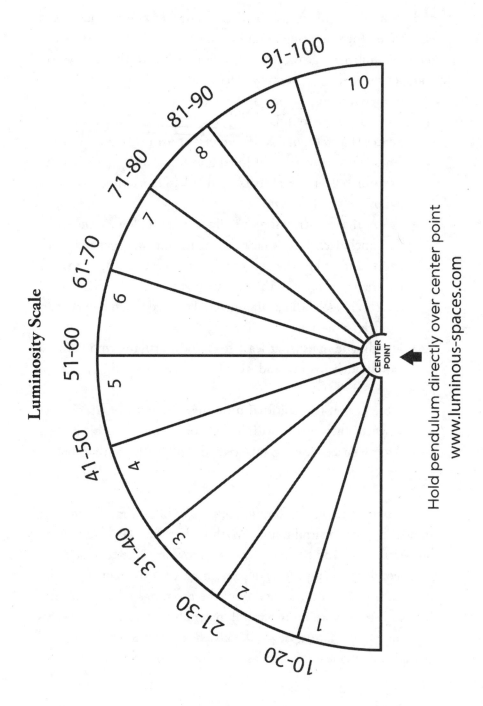

91-100 10
81-90 9
71-80 8
7
61-70
6
51-60
5
41-50
4
31-40 3
21-30 2
10-20 1

CENTER POINT

Hold pendulum directly over center point
www.luminous-spaces.com

43

and then ask again to get the actual number within that range (say, 55) on the inner ring of numbers. I use words like this: "Show me the number range on the Luminosity Scale for the energy and consciousness of _____ (item or place)."

I have tested many objects and environments, and this is a summary of what I have found:

- Spaces that felt good to me scored at least 60+ on the scale. These were usually light-filled and filled with nature in the form of the Five Elements, and inhabitants were generally happy.
- Spaces that felt draining actually scored very low on the scale. This included spaces where the inhabitants were generally unhappy and unhealthy and that did not have an abundance of nature in the form of the Five Elements.
- Objects made with natural materials scored much higher than artificial materials.
- Handmade objects, at least from local artisans who perhaps cared for their work and were fairly compensated, also scored high.
- Objects that had spiritual meaning, were well-loved, or were "owned" by someone with higher consciousness scored higher.
- After a space clearing, spaces had a higher score than before the clearing ceremony.

Although a rating of 50 might appear to be neutral, I found 60 to be the actual neutral point. Anything less than 60 is designated "life-draining," and ratings of 60 and above are "life-enhancing."

The collective impact of objects in an environment has a significant influence on the vitality of the room or building. We feel better in spaces with more natural materials that have ample access to sunlight and nature views. We also feel better in places attuned to higher consciousness, such as religious and other spiritual spaces.

READING THE LUMINOSITY SCORE OF YOUR HOUSE

If you have a pendulum or dowsing rods, or practice kinesiology, consider testing the method I've described using the scale. For the rest of you, here is a simple adaptation, based on a scale of 1–10.

Take out a deck of cards or Tarot cards and pull out cards representing Ace through Ten. (You can also cut ten pieces of paper and write 1 through 10 on them.) Place the cards facedown on a table and scatter them around.

Center yourself by sitting up straight and breathing slowly. Create balance within your body and mind. Now ask for the card that best represents the luminosity score for the energy currently in your home and pick a card.

Write the answer you received in your journal. This number can change very quickly depending on what's going on in the home and in the life of its occupants. If the number is six or greater, that's great! The energy of your home is currently life-enhancing. If the number is five or below, acknowledge that there is something that needs to shift to create a more life-enhancing space.

Other ideas: Do the space clearing and blessing on pp. 26–27 and see if the score increases. If you already did those rituals, you can ask your reading question in the past tense, such as "What was the luminosity score of my home this morning, before I did the space clearing and blessing?" You can ask for the score for yourself or an object, as well using the steps above.

We can test how much we raise the energy and consciousness of our spaces by:

- Recognizing the soul and connecting to our homes in a loving way.
- Performing a space clearing and blessing ceremony to neutralize some of the bad mojo that has built up over the years.
- Incorporating the Five Elements into our homes, which is what the balance of this book is about.

You may want to try this and see how your process impacts the energy and consciousness of the space before and after readings.

So, our environments, both natural and artificial, have a significant impact on how we feel. If we feel good in a room, we will project positive energy back into that space, which will then be received by the environment and felt by others entering that room. On the contrary, if we feel drained or angry in a room, we will fill that space with negative energy, which will then negatively impact others entering that space.

Lacking Light—Too Little Chi

Sara had recently purchased a home after separating from her husband of ten years. She contacted me to do a long-distance consultation for this California home where she was living with her son.

Sara wanted some practical help selecting colors and artwork and was also curious about her inability to make decisions and get things done. She complained about a lack of energy. She was attending college and felt her usual strong drive had disappeared. It was overwhelming.

To prepare for the consultation, Sara provided photos and a sketch of the floor plan of her home. Using her address, I was able to look at a bird's-eye view of her house with the help of Google Maps and immediately saw one major challenge: The property that her new house was built on was behind an already established home that fronted the road. This homeowner evidently built two homes in their former backyard, one behind the other. Sara's was the one in the far back. In addition, the lot was wedged between a huge shopping center parking lot on the back and side and the house in the front of her. Her property backed up to other properties on all sides, with the exception of a single long driveway to the street. She was literally and metaphorically "wedged into" this space with little room to breathe contributing to her feeling of being overwhelmed.

As Sara had moved in only a few months before and was wracked with indecision, all of the rooms in her home had bare white walls. There was no feeling of love and warmth. The little sunlight that reached her home on the front was blocked by heavy privacy curtains because of the close proximity to her neighbor's house. The light at the back of her house was blocked by a large, solid fence bounding the parking lot.

This was one of those times that I wished a client had consulted me before investing life savings on a property. Although there were major challenges, I was able to provide recommendations to attract the light and energy to her home that were symbolically keeping her from moving forward. To coax energy from the road up the long narrow driveway to her home, I suggested she place several solar lights (which are inexpensive and do not require wiring) or several moving objects, such as flags, wind chimes, or pinwheels, on the approach.

At the house, I recommended two potted plants with bright-colored flowers to flank her front door and a couple of comfortable outdoor chairs and a table for a more welcoming entry. Inside, I helped her select colors for the rooms, based on her True Nature Element and colors she loved. Knowing that she had limited time and income, I gave her suggestions on artwork to grace a few of the most important spaces in her home first for the greatest impact. To bring more light into the home, I suggested new lighter window treatments hung lower on the windows that would give her both the privacy she needed as well as more sun.

A remote space clearing and blessing ceremony that we performed together also lifted the energy of the land. These adjustments helped her get back on track in school and start her new life with her son.

Luminosity score before: 35
Luminosity score after: 62

Lacking Light—Too Much Chi

Ever since moving into her new home built about ten years earlier, Diane had had challenges finding a romantic partner and with her finances. So she gave me a call.

The house and property looked beautiful at first, however, upon closer examination there were some major concerns. The land dropped off rather abruptly behind the house, leaving the yard and house vulnerable to the frequent high winds off the waterfront. (Good feng shui is to have a hill, a group of trees, or even another home at your back to provide safety and protection from the winds.) She had already experienced a damaging hurricane while living here in which several trees toppled, thankfully missing the house.

In addition, the floor plan was odd. First, the house was large enough for a family of six, but only two people lived there: Diane and her daughter. The excessive amount of space created separation, both physically and emotionally, between mother and daughter.

The central core of the home was a transitional space between the foyer and the rest of the house. But this space had walls that were asymmetrical (greater than ninety degrees) and created angles everywhere with several doors leading to closets and a powder room. These angles were repeated upstairs in nearly every bedroom. In feng shui, angles and asymmetrical spaces are too yang for most people to feel at ease with them. They jar the senses. To add to the excessive yang energy of the home, the first floor had vaulted ceilings.

Overall, the house and land felt very chaotic and not welcoming. My suggestions included adding more yin to the home through some support in the backyard with quick-growing cypress trees, "warm" artwork and wall color to make the rooms feel more cozy, and as always, I recommended adding healthy abundant plants to boost vitality as well as create more nurturing energy.

In evaluating the change in chi from before to now, we found a shift in the right direction:

Luminosity score before: 58

Luminosity score after: 72

Feeling the Light

Christine was one of the few clients to contact me without any immediate concerns in her life. Things were going well, but she wanted to do all that she could to keep that good energy flowing with her family and life—specifically in her relationships and career. Her husband had a thriving medical practice, and she was starting her own career as a health counselor.

Their 1930s Dutch Colonial home was beautifully maintained. The landscaping was lush and alive, inviting and welcoming as I approached the front door. A small dog, Zoey, greeted me as Christine invited me in. Their three children were homeschooled by both Christine and her husband, so when I arrived, I got to meet everyone.

This house had great feng shui in that the land was welcoming and you could see and feel that the house was well-loved. The main rooms had natural light streaming in with views of mature trees and flower beds. A pond out back was home to an abundance of koi, and a turtle paddock housed four box turtles. A deck, pool, jungle gym, and hot tub rounded out the outdoor spaces in this humbly sized yard. Each space felt warm and inviting.

Some minor tweaks to their furniture layouts and landscaping, the addition of their True Nature Elements, and a space clearing and blessing ceremony with all family members participating rounded out my work with them. Even luminous spaces can use a little tweaking too!

Luminosity score before: 68

Luminosity score after: 82

So far, we've talked about energy and consciousness, what it means to raise luminosity, and why that's important for our joy and well-being. We've reviewed the fact that homes can have lower or higher levels of consciousness and what that means to the people living there. And, by now, hopefully you have connected to the energy and consciousness of your home and have a better idea of its personality, its energy, how you feel about your home, and what it needs from you. Perhaps you've checked the consciousness of your home using the Luminosity Scale. Are you ready to move forward to see how you can raise the consciousness and luminosity of your home and your soul? Let's look at bringing the light in. . . .

Chapter 4

Bringing the Light In

*Our emotional freedom, our spirit, is nurtured and supported
by those environments which are themselves alive.*
                    —Christopher Alexander, architect

In order to live fully in joy, health, and well-being, we must possess a sense of awe, respect, and connection to the natural world. We draw energy from the physical environment surrounding us. We don't just *see* our environments, we *breathe them in*. Having evolved for millions of years within the natural world, our bodies are hardwired for the things that will nurture all aspects of ourselves—body, mind, and spirit.

Hundreds if not thousands of studies are available proving the positive impact of nature in our constructed environments. Some of this information is being used in design to improve health care facilities, build better urban spaces, craft better work and education environments, and even improve some prison facilities. Now it's time for more of us to be informed and create these beneficial environments where it has the most significant impact: *in our homes*.

But how can we bring this learning inside our personal spaces? How can we cultivate a sense of connection to facilitate greater joy, health, and well-being?

I believe that the basic principles of feng shui and biophilic design are wonderful paths to follow back to nature—to ground ourselves, ignite our passions, and connect with our authentic selves.

Up until now we've focused on the *why;* now let's get down to *how* we can do this.

We are all recognizing at an increasing level that a connection to nature is an inherent need for humankind to have a sense of well-being and to further our personal and spiritual growth. And in these chaotic and frantic times, we need our connection to nature more than ever if we are to continue to grow and evolve as a species on this planet.

There are three things we can do to bring the light into our spaces: being mindful in our daily lives, tapping into the ways of nature in our lives, and bringing those ways into our homes.

MINDFULNESS IN DAILY LIFE

Probably the biggest contribution to Western culture from the East is the practice of mindfulness. Mindfulness is the first step in mature emotional and spiritual development. It is the practice of being present in the moment, to notice and observe not only the physical environment, but also the state of your emotional, mental, and spiritual health. We must first be aware of the role our thoughts and actions play in the circumstances of our lives.

You already have this practice of mindfulness deep inside, or you probably wouldn't have picked up this book. If you don't, then I am grateful that you are actively taking this step now. You are ready to move forward and take responsibility for this life you are cocreating with the world around you. This is a big choice and, for most of us, the hardest step to take.

Being mindful of our spaces is reflected in our attention to the quality of energy of our homes and our lives. We can be easily distracted with our cell phones and social media, which quickly pull us away from reflection and contemplation. Coming back to the present moment, we can more readily feel what we are creating. We wash the dishes after our meal. We put our clothes away after they've been laundered. We notice that the garden needs weeding and carve out time to do it. And in these simple tasks, we create the space to be open and present in our lives. We notice how our bodies feel and sense when something is off or when it seems just right. Practicing mindfulness opens a gateway to the inner self. We slip into the natural rhythms of the day and season in a way that connects us with a thread to our ancestors.

TAPPING INTO THE WAYS OF NATURE

While writing this book, I had a dream that Archangel Gabriel took me above the Earth. As we looked down, he pointed out all the dark spots that practically covered the land. They represented areas with poor energy and lower consciousness—areas that were devastated and dominated by the progress of humankind. However, there were some spots of light and luminosity, here and there. Places with vibrant and thriving natural habitats that have been protected and respected by human kind. These were areas of higher energy and consciousness. *I saw that expanding the light was not just a metaphor but to be taken literally, too.*

When I lecture about feng shui, I ask the audience the question: what words do you associate with feng shui? I get the same two words every time: *balance* and *harmony*. I also hear *nature* and *peace*. We instinctively know that we need more nature in our lives. So let's briefly review two wonderful systems to help us get just that.

The Five Elements

As we discussed, yin and yang are polar opposites of chi, and they are flavored by what is known as the Five Transformations of Chi, or the Five Elements. The Elements do more than represent physical matter; they also describe all the movement of life or transformations observed in nature. As with chi and yin-yang, the Five Element Theory is a significant part of Traditional Chinese Medicine, where it is recognized that illness is the result of Elemental imbalance.

The Five Elements are Wood, Fire, Earth, Metal, and Water. Their energies describe all of the cycles of life from the seasons, the times of day, and the wheel of birth-death-rebirth.

The most yin chi, Water, is symbolic of winter and the womb, where life appears to be stagnant on the outside. But inside there is vibrancy as the seeds are opening and on the move, preparing to burst through the earth and giving rise to early spring. Early spring is called young Wood—tender early sprouts, as the yang chi starts to gain hold. Late spring is called mature Wood, represented by the stable, mature trees. Yang chi continues to gain in strength until the summer solstice—the Fire Element—when the most yang chi reigns. But even in the most yang season, the yin chi is not dormant, but shows early sparks of growth. Those early seeds of yin appear as the days grow shorter and nights get cooler at the end of summer. This is the Earth Element—which is also a transitional element in feng shui. As the yin chi gains strength—called early Metal—we enter into autumn as energy contracts and conserves, preparing for the late autumn months—late Metal. At the peak of yin strength, we return to the winter solstice and the Water Element again.

It is the movement of chi emanating from each of these five stages that feeds the cycle of life in the universe.

Everything that exists in the cosmos can be classified by these Elements. Each Element has inherent qualities that can be used to describe it as it presents in the Universe—both in nature and people.

Wood

The Wood Element is typically considered the first in the cycle, since it represents the season of spring and the beginning of the New Year according to the Chinese calendar. The energy of Wood is uprising, like young tender shoots pushing up through the soil. The energy is strong and signifies vitality and flexibility.

As a species, we have evolved for millions of years in the natural world among trees and plants. Our brains are accustomed to seeing an endless variety of the color green in our environments. We associate green with health, growth, and life.

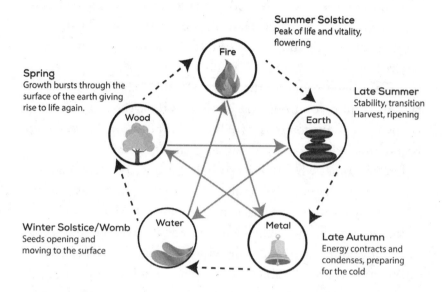

Trees, like human beings, are a bridge between Heaven and Earth. Just like us, trees receive nourishment from the earth, which is transported up through their trunks. They receive the sunlight and rain from the sky and channel it down.

Wood is connected with the directions of east and southeast; therefore, it represents sunrise, early morning, and new beginnings. As the beginning of a cycle, Wood symbolizes the archetypes of birth, rapid growth, and development. Wood is early yang energy, a masculine, creative force.

In our lives, Wood generally represents health and abundance of all good things. It is motivation and the drive to reach our goals.

Fire

The Fire Element is the most yang of the Five Elements. It represents the peak of summer and the noontime. It is in the south, as the fullest expression of the sun.

The energy of Fire is ascending like the flames of fire shooting upward. Fire is power made manifest, the fullest expression of yang energy. From the winter (Water), the germ of an idea condenses to spring when the idea shoots tendrils through the soil (Wood), until it reaches its zenith and bursts forth from the tight bud of spring.

Fire brings us light and warmth of the sun as well as the hearth. It is the magma rising up through the earth, bubbling to the surface and spilling over onto the earth. It is the cleansing blaze that whips through the forest as it feeds on the undergrowth, freeing up necessary nutrients for a thriving ecosystem.

Fire consumes what is in its path, but it is also the seeding process for new creation. The mastery of Fire distinguishes us from all other living creatures. It is excitement and connection.

In our lives, Fire generally represents our ability to be "out there" displaying our passions and skills with confidence. It also represents our reputation and the ability to be recognized for our gifts.

Earth

The Earth Element represents the energy of late summer and late afternoon, as the cycle moves past the peak of yang in Fire. Earth is a transition at critical junctures of the Five Element Cycle—traditionally, it follows Fire or summer, the peak of yang chi. In the bagua, a feng shui map used to evaluate spaces, Earth is also placed after the Water element or winter, the peak of yin chi. Earth provides a stabilizing factor that allows transformation to take place.

The Earth is our home and provides nourishment for all beings on it. Earth is the soil and sand and the rocks abundant in the planet from millions of years of compression, heat, and erosion. Earth is the horizontal surface, the stability we can rely on. Earth grounds us. It sustains life and provides a safe haven. It is the sacred ground we walk upon and completes the Cosmic Trinity of Heaven—Humanity—Earth.

The energy we get from that direct connection to the earth is life-affirming.

In our lives, Earth represents the safety and security of home. It is perseverance, follow-through, and the stable foundation on which we can build.

Metal

The Metal Element represents the energy of late autumn and evening, as energy transitions into "lesser yin." Metal is the precious minerals found deep within the earth. These minerals nourish our water, providing us with necessary nutrients—the ultimate and most coveted being gold. It represents the alchemical process of turning soil into something precious.

The cool, crisp, clean air of autumn is a perfect example of the energy of Metal—the subtle definition of the air. The Metal element is also connected to the heavens, stars, and sky. Metal is stardust. It is said to represent the spiritual path from awareness to enlightenment.

In our lives, Metal represents discernment, refinement, and strength to carry through to reach our goals. It is organization and authority.

Water

Water represents the winter and midnight, where all is still and quiet. It is the greatest yin chi. In the cycle it is connected with death and rebirth.

Of all the Elements, Water is probably most precious in that we cannot survive more than a few days without it. It quenches thirst and provides space and stillness for inner reflection. It can be deep and still like a lake, or wild and flowing like a waterfall. It matches the rhythm of our bodies to the ocean. Blood flowing through our veins is like the water flowing on the planet. Where there is water, there is life.

Water represents stillness and depth. In the *I-Ching* (also known as *The Book of Changes*), Water is called "The Abysmal." Water represents danger and mystery and often creates fear of the unseen. It has great power to overcome all obstacles and press onward. Water flows to the lowest spaces, filling them up and moving on. It has the gentleness of a trickle, yet can wear away the toughest stone.

The Water Element provides us space for reflection and contemplation. It gives us the ability to replenish and nurture ourselves. Water provides a feeling of security and rest.

The senses are all activated with the Water Element—hearing the ocean waves or the trickle of a fountain, watching the reflection of the sky in a still lake, bathing in a natural spring, and tasting pure, cool water.

In our lives, Water represents rest, stillness, rejuvenation, and contemplation. Without Water we can become parched, overstressed, and succumb to illness.

We can connect to these Elements in nature by intentionally becoming aware of them in our daily lives. By recognizing their presence we can appreciate their beauty and enhance the joy in our lives. Below is a simple exercise that I recommend you do tomorrow, if possible.

FIVE ELEMENT MINDFULNESS

Feel the quality and energy of each of the Five Elements by doing this simple exercise tomorrow:

Set your alarm to go off at 7 a.m., noon, 4 p.m., 7 p.m., and 11 p.m. At each alarm, sit quietly and notice how the energy ebbs and flows throughout the day. Observe the quality of the natural light and how it changes your view of everything around you, including the view outside and the view inside—even your inner view. I always recommend journaling your thoughts, as they often come in handy down the road.

Once you do this, you will more clearly identify with the quality of the energy of each of the Five Elements.

Five Element Relationships

In addition to embodying their own flavor of energy, each of the Five Elements has a unique relationship with each other Element. Each Element has another that creates and nourishes its energy (known as the "parent"), another Element that controls and diminishes its energy (known as the "grandparent"), and finally, an Element that drains its energy (known as the "child"). (The "grandchild" Element is another advanced relationship.)

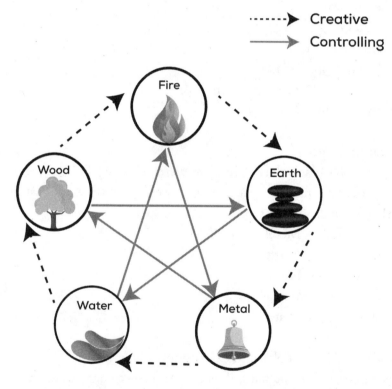

In part three, you will learn how to introduce the Elements with these cycles to promote ease, allowing you to feel the full effect of a well-balanced Element as your True Nature unfolds.

Creative Cycle

Follow the black dotted line in a clockwise direction. (This is known as the Parent/Child relationship.):

Wood fuels Fire.

Fire turns to ash/Earth.

Earth creates Metal.

Metal nourishes Water.

Water feeds Wood.

Controlling Cycle

Follow the red arrows. (This is known as the Grandparent/Child relationship.):

Water douses Fire.

Fire melts Metal.

Metal chops Wood.

Wood breaks through Earth (soil).

Earth dams Water.

Draining Cycle

Follow the black dotted line *counter*clockwise. This is the *reverse* of the Creative Cycle. (This is known as the Child/Parent relationship.):

Water drains Metal.

Metal drains Earth.

Earth drains Fire.

Fire drains Wood.

Wood drains Water.

These cycles are at play in the environment to establish balance and harmony within the natural world. And since these Elements are within us, these cycles are also at play in our own lives, as we are required to have times of ease (creative cycle), times of challenge (control cycle), and times of waning energy (draining cycle).

Biophilic Design

The second system for tapping into nature is biophilic design. Biophilic design was developed as a result of the research and collaboration of professionals in various disciplines, including neuroscience, psychology, architecture, environmentalism, and construction. It is a modern template of how we can create spaces that are more connected to nature. Up until now, biophilic design has focused on public spaces: urban centers, corporate structures, and other environments such as in the health care and hospitality fields.

The late Professor Emeritus Stephen Kellert assembled the first set of biophilic design principles, and these have been modified and adapted several times in the last decade. The list below was published by Terrapin Bright Green Consulting in the white paper "14 Patterns of Biophilic Design":

Nature in the Space
- Sensory connection to nature—visual, smell, sound, taste, and texture
- Nonrhythmic movement—such as the movement of clouds, animals, flow of water
- Thermal & airflow variability—change in temperature and airflow
- Presence of water—natural or man-made
- Dynamic & diffuse light—varying intensities of light and shadow that change over time
- Connection with natural systems—awareness of the processes of nature

Nature Analogues
- Biomorphic forms & patterns—symbolic references to contour, pattern, texture, or numerical arrangements found in nature

- Material connection with nature—use of material from local habitat
- Complexity & order—mimicking patterns found in nature such as fractals (such as found in tree branches) and sacred geometry (such as spiral of a seashell)

Nature of the Space
- Prospect—an unimpeded view over a distance for surveillance and planning
- Refuge—place of withdrawal and protection from behind and overhead
- Risk/peril—threat coupled with a reliable safeguard
- Mystery—playfulness; the promise of more information achieved through partially obscured views, entice the individual to travel deeper into the space

As you read through these basic parameters, you may recognize that much of what is called biophilic design is actually also feng shui. In fact, these principles are acknowledged in feng shui as we strive to create spaces that are in harmony with both humanity and the earth.

THE SECRETS OF A LUMINOUS HOME

Nature inherently activates our senses, bringing an aliveness into our environments.

Remember, we don't just see our surroundings; we breathe them in with all of our senses. Our senses connect with each aspect of our homes in a holistic, organic way. Nature provides us with a richness of texture, color, shape, scents, sounds, and taste that we fail to imitate.

To activate our senses, we need to take advantage of spaces with natural views in our homes. Nature provides a sense of vitality and well-being. Research shows that we feel better and are more inspired and creative when we have a view of nature. These views are restorative and boost creativity and focus. If you work primarily from home, this is a significant first step to enhancing the success of your career!

Having a connection to natural processes is believed to result in greater health and well-being. Observing and feeling the give-and-take of nature connects us to all of life and the cycles of birth and death. Some examples would be viewing the weather outside and its effects on the inside, the movement of trees in the wind, birds nesting in a tree and bees pollinating, ponding on the grass after a heavy rain, and changes in the views throughout the seasons. It is all about witnessing the ebb and flow of nature as it's reflected inside our homes and in our outdoor spaces. As I write this, I am watching the flowering of our beloved dogwood tree. Its blooms are ephemeral and long-awaited each spring.

Natural processes play a role in our homes and natural furnishings. There is no comparison between the feel of a Formica table and one made of wood. Natural materials wear beautifully with age. We appreciate the patina of copper and the weathering of bare wood. Wood, stone, and metal develop wear over use, which many affectionately call "love" for the item, like the love of a well-worn leather sofa or an antique desk.

We can enjoy local produce in season, at the peak of ripeness. I belong to a community-supported agriculture farm (a CSA), and for six months every year my family and I relish in the freshness and flavor that only local, organic produce provides us. We can nurture ourselves and our families by using organic, local ingredients when possible. We can eat according to the local seasons; for instance, we can have an abundance of root vegetables in the winter. Macrobiotics follows this principle, and it makes a lot of sense.

Even if you live in an apartment and have limited outdoor space or none at all, you can still get "out there." You can certainly do something with your *own* space that has a meaningful connection to nature. If you are fortunate to have a balcony or deck, you can enhance your space with natural materials such as wood tables, metal chairs, and twinkle lights, as well as some plants and flowers. If you do not have outdoor space, find the sunniest windows in your apartment and make a nature shrine. Create a display of plants and flowers and rotate them out with the seasons. Marigolds are hardy and great for the summer. Mums are wonderful fall plants. African violets flower year-round.

If your chosen window where you spend most of your time has limited natural light, consider creating a "garden" with some of these hardy, low-light plants: golden pothos, peace lily, ferns, anthurium, rex begonia, Chinese evergreen, dieffenbachia, snake plant, zamioc-ulcas (or ZZ plant), rubber plant, or even bamboo shoots in pebbles and water—they may need to be replaced after a year or so.

Connecting with nature is especially nurturing when you live in an urban environment. Even small touches can have a big impact on your life!

Five Organizing Principles

Nature has a clockwork all its own, and it is the Five Transforma-tions of Energy or the Five Elements. We identify with the chang-ing seasons and phases of the day. But with lighting, technology, and 24/7 schedules, we are bombarded with unnatural rhythms all day and all night. I sometimes write into the late hours of the evening, to "catch up" on what I couldn't do because of other dis-tractions during the day. Drinking caffeinated products later in the day artificially keeps us up and alert, sometimes well into the night. This disconnection from natural rhythms can be disorienting to our bodies and result in problems sleeping and eventually, illness. We can become unbalanced. Nature provides a significant respite that should not be underestimated.

The Five Elements represent five organizing principles required for a harmonious home. As you read through part two, you will find out more on these organizing principles, as well as detailed information on each of the Five Elements.

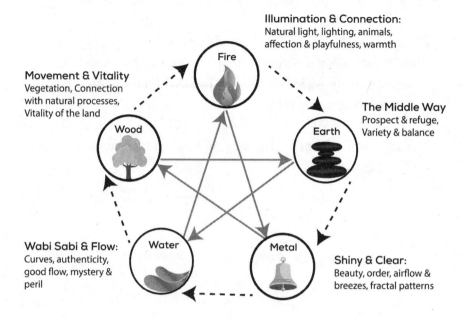

Illumination & Connection:
Natural light, lighting, animals, affection & playfulness, warmth

The Middle Way
Prospect & refuge, Variety & balance

Movement & Vitality
Vegetation, Connection with natural processes, Vitality of the land

Wabi Sabi & Flow:
Curves, authenticity, good flow, mystery & peril

Shiny & Clear:
Beauty, order, airflow & breezes, fractal patterns

Movement and Vitality—The Wood Element

Just like a tree, Wood represents our ancestors who root us to the past while enabling us to reach up to the future. It is simultaneously our foundation and our striving to achieve with new ideas and motivation.

Illumination and Connection—The Fire Element

Fire represents our enthusiasm and aliveness. It's our passion! Fire in the home gives birth to new ideas and opportunities.

The Middle Way—The Earth Element

Earth represents security and stability, balance and harmony. It is the center and mindful placement within the home.

Shiny and Clear—The Metal Element

Metal represents form and function, beauty and order. It helps us create the structures of society as well as beauty in our lives.

Wabi Sabi and Flow—The Water Element

Water is the most yin element and most precious substance for life. It is fluid and mysterious. It is associated with creativity, contemplation, peacefulness, and rest.

Let's explore this in more depth by finding out more about each of the Five Elements.

PART TWO

The Path of the Five Natural Elements

What is outside is also inside; and what is not outside man is not inside. The outer and the inner are one thing; one constellation, one influence, one concordance, one duration . . . one fruit.
—Paracelsus

We are all unique, complex individuals, having our unique experience of this world. However, there are preferences, desires, motivations, and even quirks that are common among groups of people—known as personality "types." Psychologist Carl Jung studied the recurrent types he called "archetypes" in myths and literature from cultures all over the world. He found that there appear to be universal patterns in human behavior that cut across gender, race, culture, and economic status. Combining both Western and Eastern symbols, he theorized that these archetypes—such as the Hero, the Caretaker, and the Sage—reside within a collective unconscious derived from the ancestral memory and experience common to all humankind and all have immediately identifiable traits. The Five Elements system rooted in nature also embodies and encompasses the different energy archetypes we all can identify with.

Acupuncturists Efrem Korngold and Harriet Beinfield, through their extensive study and work, recognized and developed archetypes corresponding to the Five Elements in their 1991 book *Between Heaven and Earth: A Guide to Chinese Medicine*. They recognized patterns of personality, emotion, drive, and motivation as well as patterns of illness that could be categorized by these Five Elements. They labeled each Element according to an overarching quality associated with it: Water is the Philosopher, Wood is the Pioneer, Fire is the Wizard, Earth is the Peacemaker, and Metal is the Alchemist.

> One Phase predominates, shaping and defining us as well as creating the most meaningful context for our evolution to unfold. The existential issues and questions central to our life are embodied in the symbolic archetypical figures associated with each Phase.

Understanding these Five Element archetypes helps us take a fresh look at nature's positive influence on our health and well-being. They show how nature can stimulate our relaxation response and improve our health and our lives. We can apply this wisdom by bringing the energy of the Five Elements into our inner and outer spaces.

The Five Elements restore your connection with the natural world and your True Nature. They provide a tangible way of understanding the natural forces within you, your strengths, your weaknesses or imbalances and offer a path to help restore balance and harmony—not in just a physical sense, but also on an emotional and spiritual level as well, appreciating our gifts and uniqueness with a new perspective.

I started seeing these patterns with my clients. Clients that are in balance and identifying with the qualities of their True Nature Element seem to enjoy greater well-being than those who do not. The presence of the Five Elements in their environments played a role in their own balance and harmony. Working with the Five Elements has become a perfect tool to enhance greater joy and well-being.

Looking at a couple of examples will illuminate these connections:

Susan is Water. She easily identifies with the personality traits of Water, such as creativity, independence, and a quiet demeanor. She loves working alone, yet can also work well in a group. She really appreciates Water in her environment and has a beautiful waterfall in her garden that she enjoys, as well as artwork of oceans and lakes in her home.

Michele loves that she is Wood. She is truly an adventurer, motivating and inspiring all around her, but she also has the ability to be still and grounded. She knows when to act and when it's time for observation. She lives amid a great wooded property and loves her plants and garden.

What follows is a deeper review of the Five Elements and how they serve as archetypes for energy as it moves through the land and our psyches. In addition, each chapter also contains informative tips on how to restore or support the Five Elements not just in our home environment, but in our experience with the natural world and within our inner environment.

While you are reading these chapters, see which Element resonates strongest with you. It's important to note that there will be aspects of each Element that you will identify with—that is to be expected. However, keep in mind that it's usually one Element that is predominant in our personalities throughout our life. One Element (perhaps two) is our core, our foundation from which we have been motivated and driven in our decisions in life. It helps shape our goals and desires and has formed who we are today. You may also note who you are not—and that is just as important.

For some of us, we will recognize traits of an Element from when we were young and unmarred by the judgment of others. Over the years we may have lost our sense of those qualities within us and now see undeveloped gifts waiting to be unfurled. For others, their True Natures were completely dominated by others' expectations of who they should be at a very young age. They might only be seeing their True Nature now. The qualities of our True Natures are always what feels good, what feels right, and what flows.

Another important perspective that I do hope you will get from this book is noticing the qualities of your friends and family in these descriptions. And hopefully this new perspective will bring you greater understanding and compassion in your relationships.

There will be an assessment in part three that will help you identify your True Nature Element, but you may find you already know exactly what it is when you begin reading about the Five Elements.

Also be mindful of the weaknesses of each Element as you read these chapters. Which Element do you go to when you are reacting to stressful situations and challenges? It may be the same as your True Nature Element, or it may be a different Element. Acknowledging our weaknesses is a challenging thing to do. We often bury or suppress those behaviors. They lurk in our subconscious. Perhaps we identify some of these negative behaviors with one of our parents. Be aware! We often pick up attitudes and mind-sets without consciously realizing it. But they are there nonetheless.

For instance, one trait of a balanced Earth person may be to take care of others and put the needs of others before their own. A weakness of Earth can show itself as a martyr syndrome, sacrificing for everyone in their circle while expecting grand gestures of gratitude in return. When they don't receive gratitude, they become bitter, resentful, and sometimes even vengeful. One trait of balanced Water is appreciating time alone for creative, intellectual, or spiritual pursuits. But a weakness of Water is becoming reclusive, shutting others out of their lives. The most important part of self-discovery is uncovering these behaviors and being mindful when they creep up into our everyday lives. And by the way, this Element may or may not be your True Nature Element, so it is helpful to be aware of that as well.

Chapter 5

The Wood Element

Every tree and plant in the meadow seemed to be dancing,
those which average eyes would see as fixed and still.

—Rumi

What have we learned about Wood so far?

In nature, Wood is the vegetation covering the earth, providing nourishment to all beings on the planet. Wood provides shade and oxygen. It gives a sense of vitality of the land.

Just like a tree, Wood represents our ancestors who root us to the past while enabling us to reach up to the future. It is simultaneously our foundation and our striving to achieve with new ideas and motivation. Wood can be brought into the home with live plants and flowers and can be represented in exposed wood beams, floors, and furnishings as well as window views onto vibrant nature.

As a species, we have evolved for millions of years among trees and plants. Our brains are accustomed to seeing an endless variety of the color green in our environments. Land that projects a variety of green shades denotes places with abundant rainfall, an ample water supply, and a healthy variety of food sources. We still associate the color green with health, growth, and vitality.

Trees, like human beings, are a bridge between Heaven and Earth. Just like us, trees receive nourishment from the earth, which is transported up through their trunks. They receive the sunlight and rain from the sky and channel it down. They are living, breathing, giant beings that connect us all with our divine source at a soul level. We are only learning now how to be open to their level of consciousness.

Wood is connected with the directions of east and southeast; therefore, it represents sunrise, early morning, and new beginnings. Wood represents early yang energy, a masculine, creative force, and thus the archetypes of birth, rapid growth, and development. Wood is also associated with the penetrating influence of wind: a persistent and gradual force of nature that erodes mountains and sculpts fascinating forms in nature.

Now let's have a closer look. Remember to note any words that resonate with you in our exploration of Wood so that you can refer to them for your True Nature Assessment in part three.

MOVEMENT AND VITALITY

In the same way that strong roots anchor great trees, so our emotional support system enables us to flourish. Without strengthening our roots we too become fragile brittle plants clinging to life's cliff.

—Jane Butler Biggs, Feng Shui Fusion

The energy of Wood is active and energetic; it is all about growth. Wood—which is the Element of trees and vegetation—displays the qualities of expansion and upward movement and the health and vitality of the land. When vegetation thrives, we associate it with good land. When we experience a place for the first time, we have a quick intuitive knowing about it that is a combination of the input from all of our senses. A place that is alive gives us a feeling of health and well-being.

Vitality of the Land

When feng shui was developed thousands of years ago, the most important evaluation was the quality of the land. The location of the home or village meant everything. There were two primary requirements for determining the best site: healthy, flowing water to irrigate the crops and the presence of mountains or hills to protect from harsh winds. These qualities represented the yang principles in bringing chi to a site (flowing water) and the yin principle in the containment of chi (supportive landscape).

Location continues to be the primary driver for property evaluation even today. However, given the rising population and limited open space, not everyone can wait on the best location. We build on land that has the least desirable feng shui, too. But the principles of feng shui can still be applied to achieve better energy in those locations as well. We strive for a balance of yin and yang. When there is too much yang chi, we can bring in more yin chi, and vice versa.

In most instances, roadways serve the function of bringing chi to our land rather than flowing water. If our neighborhoods are too stagnant or yin (i.e., have very little traffic), we can add movement (yang) to our property to encourage vitality with a water feature, flags, or wind chimes. If our property is too open (too yang) and lacking a "container," we can add landscaping to shore up the yin qualities we need for balance (consider the placement of any electrical device as its electromagnetic fields can be harmful to our health).

I live on a dead-end street and needed to attract more yang energy to my home, which, according to feng shui, translates to opportunities. To do this, we added a wind chime and a water fountain by the front door.

Clients of mine lived on a busy street, which had too much energy moving back and forth. At my suggestion, they added shrubs to create a physical buffer for all of this moving energy as well as developing a container for energy to gather in on their front lawn.

These principles enable us to embrace a poor site and create greater harmony. We need to manage our land to provide the greatest vitality of nature, which includes biodiversity of wildlife and plants.

THE WOOD ARCHETYPE: THE PIONEER

When it comes to personality types, the archetype of Wood is "The Pioneer"—an independent, driving force. A love of adventure, courage, and competitiveness gives Wood the motivation to spring forward into action. Wood is boundless and always on the hunt for new things to try.

Wood Is Competitive and Ambitious

Wood has the fortitude to withstand discomfort and pain on a physical or a mental level, or both, to succeed. Showing disdain for rules and daily routines, he prefers to work outside the box, challenging tradition and creating new standards. He has great courage and nothing stands in his way. He may also require constant stimulation. An active mind, as Wood has, needs complexity and challenge. However, juggling many projects may lead to extreme exhaustion.

One of the clear connections I have to Wood is this need to push forward in my career as well as my spiritual development. This clearly helps with my career goals and objectives, but not so much on the spiritual side, which requires more of the Metal and Water Elements to manifest—but we'll talk about that later!

In my work life I have what you might call "normal" goals, such as revenue, project, and publicity objectives. But every couple of years I revamp my "reach" goals. These are the plans that elicit a raised eyebrow or two from my family and friends—and *that's* when I know they are good! These goals are ones that aim so high most people would think they are completely unattainable. But my family and friends also know me better. They say "go girl!" And this is the essence of the Wood Element: reaching ever higher for the sun and the stars.

I also require the constant stimulation of projects that I am passionate about. I love having to step outside my comfort zone.

I always have no fewer than three major projects going at once. While writing this book, I am also revamping my website, developing and marketing a new workshop retreat, and teaching a new feng shui certification class. In addition, I have several other projects at various points of completion and serve on the board of directors for an industry association. I know some people's heads would blow up if they found all that on their plates. But as my mother used to say (in another reference to the Wood Element) all those years ago, "No grass grows under her feet!"

. . . But Can Be Impulsive and a Workaholic

Forging forward, Wood is prone to become obsessed with being the first and on the top of the heap. This obsession often leads Wood to work too much, putting a great strain on his ability to focus and be productive. He can be impulsive. He may get too overconfident and plow forward without thinking through the options and consequences. He can "risk it all" too easily out of the need to win at all costs.

Wood types can often neglect themselves as they get caught up in the cycle of work and constant stream of adrenaline. Becoming overly stressed and impatient, the Wood Element needs to learn to take breaks and create a regime of self-care, or they'll blow out their adrenals!

I can be impatient and impulsive in my work. I have an "it's good enough" mentality sometimes and often publish a post or a newsletter before I've had a chance to reflect, reread, and edit. When I get an idea, I want to manifest it *right now*. I like to see the immediate impact of my work. Sometimes this impulsivity is fine; other times it can be disastrous.

Back in my marketing career, one of my reports was a young, cheerful, and good-hearted woman learning a new trade. She also had a fair amount of the Wood Element. She followed my every request with enthusiasm, but whenever I reviewed her output, she was always missing at least one or two key items (let me insert here that, when reviewing someone else's work, the precision of my Metal Element kicks into high gear!). She consistently worked so quickly and sloppily that I had to keep reminding her, "Did you check your work first?" Her Wood was clearly out of balance and caused her to rush and make mistakes. The irony wasn't lost on me!

Wood Is Initiative and Vision

Wood embodies the bursting forth of spring and reaching upward for the warmth of the sun; therefore, he is associated with initiative and action. He is building the yang energy that starts the process of rebirth. The ability to see far into the distance gives him the depth and inspiration needed for proper Wood balance.

. . . Or Can Be Frustrated or Apathetic

When Wood is overworked and does not see any forward progress, he can become irritable, frustrated, and angry. When overworked, these emotions can collapse into apathy. He may give up trying entirely and sit back in a funk.

When I've worked in a team environment, I have faced instances of great frustration. As a mild-mannered person, I express my anger that way, but it's gotten to the point of apathy during a few very isolated instances. When I'm in that space, I can lose all passion for what I'm doing and it's not good for me or the project.

That's where I found myself in the early 2000s—in quite a funk! My company was going through major layoffs. It felt like we were in quicksand, taking one step forward and falling two steps back. I seriously contemplated quitting. I could not take coming into the office and having nothing worthwhile to do. For Wood types, the idea of going to work without any enthusiasm or purpose is soul-draining.

My analytical side told me to hold out, that things couldn't continue this way for too much longer; this situation would have to shift. But my Wood was craving purpose and meaning. Fortunately for me, I held on and was laid off a few months later, which came with a generous severance package. There is nothing worse for a Wood Element person than to feel unproductive and unnecessary.

Wood Is Bold and Direct

Wood branches out with confidence and self-sufficiency. He is a natural leader, forging a new path for others to follow. His path is bold and direct, with a charge of courageous heroism at times.

I saw the power of my own Wood energy at one of my freelance consulting assignments. I was asked to join a project with various stakeholders who had been struggling to come up with a solution for two years. Soon after I joined, I saw a way through but thought that perhaps I was looking at their challenges too naively. I thought, "It couldn't be as simple as that." However, after a month on the committee, I found that my perspective was correct, assumed leadership, and others fell in line. We accomplished more in a few months than they had in two years, and the project finally launched. The committee had been missing someone who could clearly see the path and direct others with a focused approach.

. . . Or Can Be Aggressive with High Expectations

Not a great delegator, he is often impatient with others and with "unnecessary" procedures, causing him to "do it himself" and in his own way. His directness can appear aggressive to others. His idea of an interesting debate might appear to be an altercation in someone else's eyes. He is so enthralled with his own thoughts that he doesn't see that there are different approaches to the challenge at hand.

I once had a boss with a brilliant mind. She was resourceful and logical and always had a clear idea of how to accomplish any task. I found her a great resource in my work. I appreciated her intelligence, directness, and point of view. However, some of my colleagues were intimated by her. She could come across as very aggressive. I witnessed many a vendor cringe as she laid into them when they didn't perform or achieve the goals as she expected. Her expectations were set so high that she was often disappointed.

Wood Is Spontaneity and Change

Wood is about flexibility, adaptability, and resilience when confronted with a challenge. He's the sprouting seed that encounters a rock—using his inborn cleverness he finds his way around any obstacle. In fact, he thrives with the idea of change and sees the adventure of possibilities.

One of my marketing positions was at a small independent agency next to the famous Flatiron Building in New York City. A couple of years after I started there, the owner sold to one of the largest communication groups in the world. Then, for the next eight years we went through a merger just about every year. I had new bosses, new clients, and new colleagues at every turn. We consolidated and expanded, and with every new venture I felt great excitement. Change, at least in my career, has always been fun and brought about new opportunities for learning and growth.

. . . Or Can Be Inflexible and Stubborn

Too much Wood can make one inflexible, stubborn, and unable to see other viewpoints. His stubborn attempt to go his own way can lead him into a dead end, unable and unwilling to think of other options.

The archetype of Wood (Pioneer) is evident among the world explorers, industrial tycoons from the late nineteenth and early twentieth centuries, modern-day entrepreneurs, corporate leaders, and typical of many professional athletes.

Wood types may have some of these facial/body features: a square jaw, well-developed eyebrows, large brow bone, or indented temples.

He tends to be either tall and lanky (like a tree) or short and compact (like a gymnast) with greenish/brown undertones to skin.

Physical symptoms associated with Wood in Excess are an abuse of stimulants like coffee and chocolate, which provide the adrenaline rush that Wood craves. The Wood personality is prone to high blood pressure, vertigo, accidents, and neck tension. Too little Wood can lead to a weak constitution. Weak Wood cannot stand on his own, like a floating weed. He is indecisive, unsure, and lacking confidence. He is scattered and distracted. "Wishy-washy" or lacking any strong opinions, weak Wood can feel humiliated.

Wood's home is filled with new electronic gadgets, of which he is very fond, and his work is spread all over the dining room table. He has a home gym (or wishes he did!) and a great home office where he spends lots of his time.

Strengths and Weaknesses

Strengths—Endurance, leadership, seeks and loves challenge and competition, courage, does well under pressure, requires novelty, action-oriented, great initiative, flexible and adaptable to challenges, resilient, quick thinking on his feet, clever and resourceful, breaks rules.

Weaknesses—Intolerance, recklessness, impatience, boredom with follow-through, arrogance, volatile emotions such as frustration and anger, impulsivity, erratic behavior, deviousness, ambivalence, abuse of stimulants and sedatives, hates feeling constrained.

Wood is nourished by the Water Element. In fact, the Chinese often use flowing water to represent prosperity. Wood is controlled or chopped down by the ax of the Metal Element. For instance, the ordered trait of Metal reigns over the impulsive, dynamic quality of Wood, making it pause and contemplate. Wood builds up the Fire Element; therefore, its chi is drained by Fire. Wood, in its path to glory, pushes aside and sprouts through the soil of the Earth Element; therefore, it controls Earth.

In our lives, Wood generally represents health and our family and ancestors (what has come before us). It also represents wealth, prosperity, benevolence, and abundance of all good things.

THE WOOD ELEMENT IN THE HOME

Bringing the Wood Element into our home invites flexibility and change. It fosters creativity and productivity. Wood ushers in motivation, action, and initiative.

Adding fresh live plants and flowers into your home is the most powerful way to stimulate the chi of Wood. Plants generate fresh air, add moisture (especially helpful in dry climates and seasons), absorb harmful electromagnetic energy from electrical wiring and appliances, as well as promote the unconscious energy of productivity, growth, and new life.

Many clients have given me the excuse that they don't have a green thumb—they just kill their plants. I encourage you to take up a nurturing mindfulness practice with your houseplants—or your garden for that matter! The benefits are great, including beauty in your home as well as cultivating a more caring attitude toward all of life.

Bring inside some found objects from nature representing Wood such as a piece of driftwood on a shelf in the summer, a basket of pinecones on your hearth in the fall, or a vase with forsythia branches in spring. A friend of mine created a unique banister for the main staircase in her home with a large sturdy piece of driftwood she found on the beach. It's simply gorgeous!

The colors of Wood are in the green family, from pale sage to bright lime green to deep forest. Wood shapes mimic the trunk of a tree, tall and vertical. Columns, pillars, and upright rectangles are all shapes of Wood. Wood artwork is composed of forest scenes, trees, and flowers.

Wood Is Initiative and Vision

If you are a Wood type, create a space for creativity and productivity—a space to start and manage projects to fruition (a home office, craft room, or garden shed). A long-distance view from a window in your home will allow you to look ahead and visualize where you are going and where you want to go. If your windows are obstructed by heavy drapes or blocked by overgrown shrubs, you cannot have that vision.

Create a vision board to help manifest your dreams and goals. Place it somewhere prominent so you are reminded of your vision every day. I have had a vision board for the last two years, and almost everything has manifested in my life, including this book! In fact, I recently removed items and replaced them with new goals and ambitions. The board sits next to my desk so that I am surrounded by the magic of my future.

Wood Is Bold and Direct

Our homes should have a direct, easy flow of energy throughout. Sometimes, things clog up our spaces and make it challenging to get anything done, which is a nightmare for Wood Element types.

Clear away paths in your hallways and move any furnishings that might complicate getting from one place to another in your home. If there is a table that you are constantly bumping into as you round a corner, move it!

Go outside and check the pathway to your front door. Is it easy to find from the street? Lighting or flags will mark the path for easy access. Do you have house numbers on your property? Are they readable from the street? It is amazing how often I visit clients' homes to find there is no house number or only one covered up by overgrown landscaping.

Make sure that you have direct and simple pathways inside and outside your home to invite a stronger Wood Element.

Wood Is Spontaneity and Change

Create a space where you can spontaneously switch out the artwork or move furnishings to change up the environment. Oftentimes, just being able to sit in a new spot can bring about a new perspective. A new view creates a "new view!" This really can inspire your creativity on a challenge or a new project.

When I moved my home office from the awful, dormered upstairs spare room it was in for ten years to the front room (formerly the living room) in my house, it changed everything! It opened up my view, my vision, and provided the expansiveness I required in my forward-thinking career!

THE WOOD ELEMENT IN THE GARDEN

The Wood Element in the garden allows for dynamic change and vision. Spend some time in your outdoor spaces. Notice if your garden has an area that is free-form as well as structured—a good balance. Or is there too much Metal controlling the Wood of the garden? Is it tidy yet uninspiring? Have you imposed structure on it that is not congruent with the land? Let the land speak for itself. What does it want to have in this space? What is appropriate for the climate, the form of the land, access to natural light?

All vegetation is considered the Wood Element, but when we look at integrating the energy of the Five Elements, Wood is particularly represented by the trees. It is a well-known fact in real estate that properties with abundant mature trees command higher prices than their treeless counterparts.

Prior to my current home, we lived on a lot roughly the same one-quarter-acre size standard for suburban properties. But there is a huge difference between the two. Our old land had one large oak and one small dogwood that we planted when we moved in. It had a score of 55 on the Luminosity Scale. Other than that, there were a few overgrown shrubs and a small garden in the front. In contrast, our current land has over thirty trees, including oak, maple, dogwood, pine, holly and cedar. Its energy is an 84 on the scale. It's like night and day to the other lot.

My first recommendation if you want to add Wood to your outdoor space is—you guessed it—plant more trees. Be sure to plant several varieties of trees and shrubs for a nice yin-yang balance: think about different heights, shapes and colors of leaves, and flowers. Depending on your geography, consider planting evergreen as well as deciduous, so that your land has perpetual green as well as the beautiful changing colors of the leaves in the fall months.

Consider adding Wood structures in your yard, including fencing, gates, decks, an arbor, trellises, etc. Items made from raw, natural wood are the most beautiful and evoke the true energy of Wood. Build a garden for flowers or vegetables or both! Plant flowers that attract wildlife so that you can enjoy the activity from your desk, kitchen sink, or sunroom.

Remember, Wood is the color green, so all the green in your garden represents it. Wood is symbolized by tall, vertical forms. Arborvitaes and cypress trees are perfect examples of the Wood shape.

THE WOOD ELEMENT IN NATURE

Engage your senses with the practice of forest bathing. Forest bathing was created by the Japanese government in the 1980s. While wrestling with soaring suicide rates, the government did research that showed that engagement with trees promotes health and well-being. Forest bathing simply requires a mindful, conscious walk through a wooded or forested area in a slow deliberate way to help calm your senses and restore peace of mind. Here are some ideas from forest bathing to help you connect with the Wood Element in your daily life:

Take a walk in the woods or a garden and gently touch leaves and flowers, smell, become aware of all of the shades of green in your view, and awaken all of your senses.

Time of Day—Be present and aware at dawn as the sun rises. This is the energy of Wood. Notice the quality of the light as it bathes everything around you.

THE SACRED

Connecting with Trees

Humanity has long been intrigued by the awesome energy of trees. The druids knew they were sacred and worshipped among tree groves. There is a strong magnetic energy field around trees—the larger and older the tree, the stronger the field.

We can also restore harmony to the land by doing energetic space clearings and blessing rituals. Although it is best to perform these rituals prior to work on the land, we are able to, with the grace of the natural world, provide humble apology and express love and gratitude for the bounty of nature. Thank the trees for their shade and beauty and for shelter and food for the wildlife that brings the land to life. Give thanks to the wildlife for their vitality and beneficial energy—to the birds and their song, to the bees and their pollination, to the flowers and food crops, to the many insects and animals that are part of a vibrant ecosystem.

CONNECTING TO THE TREES

Here is a simple exercise, similar to one I learned on a retreat:

- Take a walk in the woods or notice a tree in your yard that seems to call out to you. Approach the trunk, rub your hands together and hold out your palms two to three inches from the bark. Ask for permission to connect with the tree. Very rarely have I received a "no"—which is usually some kind of intuitive signal. Be aware of what occurs when you ask. Sway and feel the energy interchange. Be still and you may "see" or hear a message from the tree. You can also ask the tree spirit a question.

- Face a tree and place your hands on the trunk. Make the intention to release any negative thoughts into the tree. The tree receives this energy unharmed and absorbs it.

TREE MEDITATION

- Sit with your back to a tree. Calm yourself with your breath.
- When you are ready, imagine your spine merging with the trunk of the tree.
- Imagine you feel the roots of the tree reaching down to the cool, moist soil, pulling up minerals from the earth and connecting with the energy of all other trees in the forest or surrounding area. Feel their breath. Feel the gravity and being rooted to the earth.
- Imagine that you are taking the journey up the trunk of the tree with water and nutrients. Feel yourself going up.
- Go up still higher, to one of the large branches, out to a smaller branch, and so on, until you reach a leaf.
- You are now in the leaf. Feel the sun overhead and the brilliant green of the leaf.
- See the nutrients and water nourishing every cell. Feel how it is to be part of this tree.
- Explore, and experience the joy. Be playful.
- Feel the sun as its warmth interacts with the water, nutrients, and cells in the leaf.
- When you are ready, go back to the branches and find your way down the trunk to your body.
- Make small movements with your fingers, feet, head. Feel your body.
- When you are ready, open your eyes and feel cleansed and joyful!

CASE STUDIES

The Boldness of Liz

I met Liz at one of my feng shui workshops. She was transitioning from the corporate world to being a solo entrepreneur in the graphics design field. In addition to her career, she had been married to Ben for several years and wished to start a family.

I immediately saw that Liz was Wood. She talked about her new work with great boldness and confidence. She had no qualms with stating that she knew she would be very successful. A self-proclaimed workaholic, Liz often had five projects going at once and found it very challenging to take any time off. In fact, she often worked late into the night, which inhibited her intimacy with Ben and their ability to get pregnant.

As is typical with strong Wood types, Liz broke the rules in her design work. She was avant-garde, a bit of a pioneer, and strong-willed when it came to her work. And this is why some were attracted to work with her. She was also very competitive and somewhat impulsive, and she sometimes took on clients without vetting them to see if they were a good match, which wound up causing her great pain. Disputes with clients were happening often, and she had several clients that didn't pay.

She often found herself frustrated and impatient with clients and vendors that didn't fully "get" her designs. This created a lot of stress in her day-to-day life. As often happens with strong Wood personalities, her Metal was very strong, too. She found it hard to find vendors with similar standards and dedication. Liz felt personally assaulted when clients expressed their own opinions, and their criticism was hard for her to take.

Regarding the fertility issue, Liz couldn't understand why she couldn't get pregnant. For her, everything came easy. She felt in full control and in charge of her success in work, yet, with this desired pregnancy, she experienced great anxiety and frustration.

As often happens with strong Wood types, dealing with emotions and feelings seemed foreign to her. In order to feel in charge again and avoid processing her emotions and feeling the pain, Liz buried herself in more work, which just perpetuated all the above challenges.

When visiting her lovely home, I noticed that there were several home projects that were in various stages of completion. Wood types love to start new projects but often have trouble with follow-through. This can create an environment of chaos and frantic energy. I suggested that they pick one project at a time and finish it, so that the environment would provide more stability and calmness to reduce her stress.

Her husband was a collector and had lots of clutter that Liz complained about. I recommended to her husband that clearing out and organizing his stuff would unblock some obstacles they were both feeling in career and family. The metaphor of blocks with fertility issues made an impression on both of them.

In Liz's home office, I recommended a water fountain to nourish her Wood Element, since Water is parent to Wood, and a few plants to reinforce her Wood, as well as to provide fresh air and mitigate some of the electromagnetic fields from the computer equipment.

I also suggested that she add the Wood Element to their bedroom, which would benefit both her and her husband (he was Fire). So she purchased a beautiful woven sea grass headboard and got new bedding with a botanical print. I suggested that she connect with the trees on her property with the Tree Meditation, and she loved the idea. She started to do a daily meditation at my recommendation and found that it gave her a great sense of peace throughout the day.

I worked with Liz for several years, and I'm glad to say that she and her husband had a beautiful baby boy last year. She found her balance and tempered her impulsiveness. She is a successful designer!

Surrounded by Trees

Kim's house was practically surrounded by a forest. It was set back on property filled with white oak, red maple, eastern white pine, and yellow birch.

It didn't surprise me that her True Nature Element was Wood. Her career was very important to her. She was ambitious, often took leadership roles, and was good at planning and training others. In fact, she had just accepted a promotion to become one of the top administrators for the college where she worked.

As is typical with Wood types, she relishes change. She sees it as an adventure with new possibilities. The desire for change didn't just get expressed in her career, but also in her desire to renovate and redecorate her house. In fact, she wanted to look for a new home. Her husband, a strong Earth Element type, kept her grounded to the status quo. Although Earth and Wood are in the Controlling cycle in Five Elements Theory, when in balance, they can have a wonderful complementary energy. While Wood can be impulsive, Earth is the stabilizer. And when Earth becomes too stuck, Wood provides the impetus for proper movement.

In our conversation, Kim said that time management was a challenge for her. They used to go to the gym four days a week in the early morning hours. Career stress was getting the better of her and she regretted that she had gotten away from that habit and wanted to start doing yoga. For Wood types it is often hard to schedule time away from work and to slow down.

While we were touring the home, she showed me a lovely family room that had been designed a few years before by an interior designer. Although the designer had gotten her approval on all of the decisions for the room, Kim was unhappy with the result. When out of balance, Wood can be indecisive and then regret decisions.

As is typical for a Wood person, her home office, shared with her husband, was center stage in the house. They used the formal living room for their work, which had great views out to the property.

While discussing her Wood Element, we both noticed that almost all of the artwork in the house had a tree or flower theme. The exception was the artwork behind her desk—a scene selected by her designer. She didn't feel any connection with the piece.

I recommended that she get a water fountain for the foyer to support her Wood nature (Water feeds Wood) and contribute to a soothing environment while she worked. I also suggested that she replace the artwork she wasn't attracted to with one representing the Wood Element. She replaced it with a beautiful piece with—you guessed it—a stand of trees! She felt so supported and nourished by it.

In addition, I recommended they add the Wood Element in their bedroom, which would nourish both Kim and her husband. Kim purchased and hung several prints with trees and flowers above their headboard and added a new bedspread with a botanical print.

Instead of looking for a new home, they compromised by making some upgrades to their current house including a new front facade and a small porch to merge the inside and outside spaces in their home and enjoy their private "forest," as well as serving as an inviting portal for guests.

ACTIVATE YOUR WOOD POWER!

Too much Wood in our personalities will show up as an impulsive, impatient, and perhaps angry demeanor along with an inability to hear others' ideas and look for alternative solutions. There may be a fear of losing power and position. When Wood is in excess, it can be dominating. When Wood collapses, it loses confidence and decisiveness. Collapsed Wood leads to apathy and dependence. We may also feel helpless and humiliated. Clients with low or collapsed Wood are typically unmotivated and have low self-esteem. They can be either irritable and arrogant or scattered and frightened.

Balanced Wood is strong, ambitious, and motivated. His competitiveness requires others to "up their game" and raises everyone up. The Pioneer is visionary, resourceful, and resilient, able to adapt and find solutions to every challenge. Wood's courage and penchant for adventure brings us to new shores and enlightens our society with new discoveries and ideas.

Want to reclaim your Wood power? On a personal level, you can also identify with the energy of the Wood Element through your clothing. Wood loves sporty, athletic-style clothing as well as business casual. Consider plant-based fabrics such as bamboo and cotton, as well as patterns such as stripes and floral. Chunky wood accessories also represent this Element.

Bring the Wood Element into your home with fresh, healthy plants. Paint your bedroom green. Move your favorite seat so that you can have long-distance views of nature for vision and insight. Get in touch with a big old tree and become aware of its wonderful energy—perhaps ask a question and listen for a message. Create that vision board and open to that vision. Be bold and start new projects that you've been talking about for the last few years! Be more spontaneous—have an adventure! We all need the initiative and courage that the Pioneer brings to our lives!

Chapter 6

The Fire Element

Isn't it time to turn your heart into a temple of fire?

—Rumi

Now, let's look at what we know about Fire.

Fire is the most yang of all the Five Elements. Our sun is the primal symbol of Fire. For millennia, cultures worshipped the sun and its benevolent spirit as a deity. It is the Earth's primary energy force and provides light, heat, and the pull that keeps the Earth on its orbit. Vegetation requires the light from the sun for photosynthesis. Our bodies absorb this same light into our skin, which aids in regulating hormones, mood, and sleep. A lack of natural light can lead to depression and mental illness.

Fire is luminous, hot, and intense. Its power is all-consuming. It's associated with hot, bright, loud, and masculine energy. It is the brilliant light during the peak of the sun at noon and also the summer solstice. It is the fullness and ripeness of life. It is the magma rising up through the earth, pushing to the surface, and spilling over onto the earth, consuming all in its path. It is the cleansing conflagration that whips through the forest as it feeds on the undergrowth, freeing up necessary nutrients for a thriving ecosystem. The Fire Element symbolizes the sun as it travels across the sky. Fire is associated with south on the compass.

Fire brings us the warmth of the sun as the heart of our solar system, but also of the hearth as the heart of the home. It is the warmth of a campfire that brings people together. It is the flicker of the flame that can inspire intimacy and passion.

The energy of Fire ascends like flames rising upward to the heavens. It is the fullest expression of yang. As the Five Element cycle moves from Water representing winter and the greatest yin energy into the Wood Element, the sprouting birth of yang energy and spring bursting forth from the seeds deep underground expands fully into its own and on to the Fire of summer, this Element is power made manifest.

Fire teaches us that power results from connecting and merging, rather than dominating or withdrawing. True power gives us grace and balance.

As we dive deeper into Fire, remember to note any words that speak to you for your assessment in part three.

ILLUMINATION AND CONNECTION

Fire symbolizes illumination of all varieties and connection with others in our spaces. It represents the sun, or natural light, as well as artificial light. Called "dynamic and diffuse light," Fire gives us varying intensities of light and shadow that change over time. With light we get heat or thermal variability. Fire is reflected in the sound of wildlife, specifically birds and the buzzing of bees, outside our windows. But Fire is also about affection for our spaces and connecting from a heart-centered place.

Sunlight makes us feel positive and energetic. The movement of the sun across the sky is a reminder of the Fire Element. It connects us to nature through the cycles of the day. We can tell the approximate time of day by the quality and strength of the light in our homes. Morning light has a freshness to it with the full promise of a new day. At noon, as the sun peaks, the quality of light becomes more pointed and focused like a laser. There is great illumination and clarity—no shadows. The waning of the sun in the afternoon again shifts the energy with golden light. As with the sunrise when the sun is lower in the sky, it passes through denser atmosphere that absorbs more of the blue and green wavelengths, resulting in a golden-reddish glow.

THE FIRE ARCHETYPE: THE WIZARD

The Fire Element is known as the archetype of the Wizard who has the ability to bring ideas to fruition. After the seed of an idea (Water) and the emergence of the tender young shoot (Wood), Fire blooms and makes things happen!

Fire Needs Affection and Connection

Fire is formless and aspires to the heavens. He has an insatiable need for contact and merging with others. He reaches out, just like a flame, to connect with others. He wears his heart on his sleeve, and this ability to be so vulnerable is often captivating. People respond to Fire—they feel his sincerity and warmth.

Fire is about confidence and the ability to connect to others. He speaks and moves quickly and with a surety that comes from an open heart, self-acceptance, and love. Fire feels compassion and a lack of judgment emanating from a balanced and open heart chakra.

Others love his enthusiasm and light. Fire people are often laughing and living life to the fullest. They love being involved with groups, be it with work, community, special interests, or all of the above! They have a large group of friends, often from all different areas of their life.

. . . But Fears Smothering

Fire people love being surrounded by a group of friends, but sometimes too much can be too much. If they overcommit, they may feel stuck with responsibility and drudgery. Drudgery is the worst thing for Fire! They can feel smothered just as if too much Earth (dirt) gets swept up into a Fire, it goes out. Fire needs to flee before any chance of being smothered.

When overwhelmed, Fire people often cannot discern between their own emotions and others'; their feelings can overwhelm them and create anxiety and confusion. When life suddenly shifts their reality, they can become fearful and agitated. They may sense a loss of identity and isolation. This can lead to melancholy and passivity.

Fire Is Laughter and Fun

Fire is enthusiasm, joy, and passion for life. An extrovert, he lives life with gusto! Burning brightly, he can be boisterous and is usually the life of the party.

According to Western astrology I am a Leo—a fire sign that is represented by the sun. Before I even understood what that meant, I was a quintessential Leo child. My older sister and brother would nudge me during family pictures and say "stop that fake smile!" But what they didn't realize is that it wasn't a fake smile. It was my smile—big and toothy—happy to be in the spotlight and in front of a camera. A genuine, big smile is a sure sign of Fire.

Fire Is a Performer

In our lives, Fire generally represents our ability to be "out there" displaying our passions and skills with confidence. It also represents our reputation and the ability to be recognized for our gifts.

My childhood friend John got a taste of the stage at an early age. His first experience was being picked to represent the first grade at mass. He read a passage from the Bible as the microphone cracked and screeched, but his parents were so pleased. From that point on he was comfortable on a stage. He entered talent shows, sang in the school chorus, and joined every club (yes, there were several) that related to singing. He hadn't sung on stage in years, but while in Paris last year, he volunteered to be the first karaoke competitor of the evening when visiting a youth hostel with his daughter. Fire people love to perform.

John is now a teacher, and if you don't think that teaching is akin to performing, think again! Fire is about connecting with others, often on a large scale.

. . . But Fears Criticism

Although Fire people love to be in the spotlight, watch out if they feel unloved and unwanted. Fire craves praise from others to feel substantial and accomplished. They feel kind words from others as intensely as the sun's rays. But this can all be shattered by one critical word. Requiring constant outside validation is a sign of low self-esteem, Fire needs to cultivate self-respect by acknowledging his own achievements.

Throughout his life John has been challenged to grow beyond needing constant approval from his peers. Without that approval, he has second-guessed himself—although this sometimes serves a good purpose to slow him down a bit and has saved him from making impulsive mistakes (Wood!). Fire has a soft heart and needs attention and admiration.

Fire Loves Passion and Drama

As in the drama of a sunrise or sunset, Fire is center stage, the focus of attention. Hypnotizing all who come within his grasp, he exudes personal magnetism and charm. Fire people love drama, of course, and they are very enthusiastic and passionate, whatever their interests are. They love the novelty of new things, new ideas, new people, and new projects. They throw themselves into whatever is the topic of the day with great gusto!

Fire goes all out! He gives and demands a lot from his circle. Fire takes on a lot, volunteers for this and that, but often does not recognize that this one more thing will push him over the edge. He must learn to contain his power or be consumed by it, like a forest fire laying waste all of the resources of the land.

John gets very passionate about his teaching. His work touches so many. He gets tons of ideas (flowing Water), believes that they all are valid and worthy of his immediate attention (lots of Wood), and throws himself into each one with abandon, chunking through each project. He is excited, filled with adrenaline, and very productive.

. . . But Often Isn't Enduring

But this impulsive project-starting often ends with confusion and melancholy. Fire people can be all-in with a new friendship or romance, and then when the novelty wears off, they are on to the next person. The same goes for work projects: they are not great long-term project managers. And yes, the same goes for home projects. Have you ever seen a house where there are maintenance and renovation projects in all stages throughout the space? Or the one with the paints and canvases or piles of photos and odds and ends for a scrapbooking project everywhere? These are Fire people whose passions are represented with unfinished projects!

John is challenged to keep his momentum going. At the beginning he's all-in, but at some point, he realizes that this project or goal doesn't really fit with his long-term strategy. He can then lose all momentum and have no desire to continue. What is hard to learn is that the enthusiasm and excitement are always the same at the beginning. It's only a few weeks or sometimes months in that his motivation peters out and he's stuck with a partly done project that wasted money, time, and energy. But when the project is truly a winner, he's in it for the long haul (that's the Earth in him).

Fire Lights Others Up

It's palpable: people love being around Fire because they feel the light. There is joy and exuberance. Fire's light and heart-centeredness are often a catalyst for others to see things that were obscured before. Fire can bring people out of the doldrums and raise them up, even momentarily. Fire can be that lightning strike that briefly illuminates all around it. Fire can activate and energize. Fire provides the clarity and illumination of transcendence.

The archetype of the Wizard is the stage performer, the court jester, and the traveling salesman. Fire people command attention and create quite a gathering. Their passion and enthusiasm attracts energy like a moth to a light. The Wizard is often found in performers, successful speakers and salespeople, and any occupation that requires high energy and connection.

The Wizard's eyes are his most dramatic trait. They gleam. He often has red or curly hair, or perhaps it's spiky or the top of the head is bald (Fire burns it off!). He often has a cleft chin and dimples, with pointed tips to the corners of the eyes. He is quick to smile and laugh and has quick movements and speech. His skin has freckles and a pinkish tone (regardless of race).

John fits the physical attributes of Fire, with a reddish caste to his hair, freckles, and reddish tone to his skin. His fiery eyes sparkle (especially when he's being mischievous), and his laughter is contagious!

Too little Fire results in a weak heart, low blood pressure, fainting, and anemia. With too little energy, Fire can be lethargic and chill easily. On the contrast, too much Fire is too much heat. It can result in an enlarged heart, profuse perspiration, a flushed face, chest pains, and dry, painful eczema.

Fire's home is often a place of parties and overnight guests. He decorates in dramatic color schemes. He loves to collect things, and his home is filled with them everywhere in a rather haphazard fashion.

Strengths and Weaknesses

Strengths—Communication, charisma, extrovert, great at assembling a team to fill in gaps, has vision, often has great clarity on the end goal, great enthusiasm, very intuitive, follows hunches, a great inspirer, speaker, performer, great at motivating others, generous.

Weaknesses—Can become anxious, doesn't know how to pace himself, may burn too brightly and then collapse (burnout), not a good planner, can be overwhelmed/become bored with details and follow-through, can be flirtatious.

Fire is nourished by the Wood Element. Fire is controlled or doused by the Water Element. For instance, Water's need for independence can reign over the desire to always be surrounded by people and to be accepted, both of which are qualities of Fire. Fire burns and turns the Wood to ash or soil (Earth), therefore Fire's chi is drained by Earth. When Fire burns hot, its flames reach out in all directions, burning everything in its path, melting the hardness of Metal. Therefore Fire controls Metal.

In our lives, Fire represents illumination and clarity. It contains the ability to radiate the light from within. In an outer sense, Fire symbolizes being "out there" in the public, on the stage, front and center. Fire represents fame and recognition, being noticed. It also represents our need to belong to a community, connection, and a sense of purpose.

THE FIRE ELEMENT IN THE HOME

It is important to take advantage of locations in your home that have great natural light. Aligning with the cycles of light throughout the day makes us happier and more productive. Use these spaces for the bulk of your daytime hours. I'm a big proponent of "mobile" home offices. I work in the kitchen in the morning, move out on the deck in good weather, and then to my home office to take advantage of the late afternoon sun. And I get a bonus *every day*: I see the sunset and changing skies of early evening! However, this doesn't mean that I suggest having your work pile up all over the home. I do believe it is important to have a home base for your office where you keep your files, books, and electronic equipment.

Take the time to observe the quality of sunlight throughout the day. Test yourself: at some point during the day, without referring to a clock, look up at the sky and guess approximately what time it is. You might be surprised how close you are! Our dormant attention to nature can still be awakened.

Besides sunlight, the Fire Element is at its most powerful through real fire. If you have a fireplace, use it and enjoy the warmth and connection it provides. Perhaps add some candles in your home to instill intimacy and romance—but please stay away from wax and artificially scented candles, which are a health hazard!

Artificial lighting is one of the challenges in personal spaces. Many people do not realize the importance of proper lighting to their health and well-being. There are many aspects of lighting to consider: the number of fixtures, type of fixtures, placement of fixtures, wattage of bulbs, and finally the color/type of bulb to use. These variables open up the potential to create a room that is too yang or too yin. A good indication of proper lighting is a room that feels good to you for its primary purpose. For instance, if a space is to be used for reading books, then you actually enjoy reading a book here. If a room has improper lighting, it will definitely be one you don't enjoy being in!

Recessed or overhead lights cast strange shadows in a room. They lower the energy and can drain your energy. The color of the light is most important. The cool, bluish light from fluorescent bulbs and some LEDs and CFLs, as well as electronic devices, contribute to poor health. Their harsh illumination poorly mimics sunlight and inhibits the production of melatonin, which keeps us in a wakeful state, unable to sleep or rest.

To create the best lighting plan for a room, consider the primary function of the room and the time of day you will spend there. A variety of lighting to mimic nature is the best option, including filtered or diffused light (using shades), reflective light (lamps or sconces reflecting light off ceiling or wall), warm light (mimicking fire), and task lighting. Consider replacing dark lamp shades with light-colored ones to brighten up a room. Changing the wattage and color of your bulbs is sometimes all you need to get the right ambience.

Light brings warmth, but warmth is also given off by our heating systems, both natural and artificial. This is one of the most important factors in studies of environmental psychology: the ability to control the temperature of our spaces and how that impacts our sense of well-being.

People and animals are expressions of the Fire Element because we are alive. If you have several people in your home, there is probably lots of activity, coming and going, moving the chi around.

If you live alone or with a partner and have a quiet life, you can bring more Fire into your home with a pet or two. Pets provide us with lots of energy, affection, and the playfulness associated with Fire. They help to distribute the chi with their movements around the home. I had a client who wanted to open himself to a romantic relationship. My intuition was that he could really benefit from a pet—specifically, a cat—to open his heart. When I mentioned this to him, he said that he had actually been considering getting one, and he did after our consultation.

Using the colors of Fire is another way to stimulate activity: red, orangey-red, as well as shades of brilliant purple and pink. The color red has a powerful energy so a little can go a long way. One signature red chair can be a brilliant way to make a statement in any room. Depending on the purpose of the room, use these colors sparingly. In rooms where you want a more restful tone such as bedrooms, a study, or a meditation space, a few accents of color are good, perhaps just on one wall, or in some fabric or a few throw pillows.

The shapes that represent Fire are essentially all things "pointy," such as stars, triangles, pyramids, and zigzag patterns. You can find these in fabric or objects in your room. Fabrics that are considered

Fire are primarily from animals, such as silk, satin, leather, hide, fur, and other animal skins. The Fire Element can be brought in through artwork depicting any scenes with the sun, fire, people, and animals.

Fire Is Affection and Connection

As we discussed in chapter two, having a connection with your home's consciousness is vital, and a sort of affection from both sides will enable a healthy relationship to grow.

The kitchen is considered a Fire room in feng shui because it's where we place the oven and stove. A fireplace invites a cozy, warm feeling in any room, but for those without one, or even those with, candles can contribute to the warm ambience. In the Danish practice of *hygge* (pronounced "hoo-gah" and loosely translated to "cozy"), the main ingredient to a space is the ambience of the light (fire) in a room.

What could be more endearing than a dog or cat in our homes? Having had both in my life, I know they become an important extension of the family. Many people only share their homes with a pet. They offer us unconditional love and affection and provide many an opportunity for lots of furry hugs!

Fire Is Laughter and Fun

Do you want to jump-start Fire energy in your home? Host a party! Music and laughter lift the joy in your home and heart immediately! Laughter and humor are vital to our sense of joy in life. In my own house, we had a much-used family room and a vacant living room. When our children were little, we decided to use the living room as our "ballroom" for music and much laughter. I can still feel the reverberations of all that joy there!

There is inherent playfulness in nature. Just watching the birds and squirrels on my property puts a smile on my face. Our pets make us laugh every day!

We can also incorporate fun spaces in our home with color or artwork. Lightness and joy can be expressed in our homes through artwork, colors, unexpected objects, or "secret" nooks. Whimsy is the spark of inspiration and the spice of life! Bring more warmth from the heart and playfulness into your home through a choice of bold colors, energetic artwork such as party scenes and celebrations, or art from a child, as well as eclectic objects from cultures around the world. A fun wind mobile by the front entry not only creates positive movement for chi to enter your front door, but will add a lighthearted touch that welcomes visitors. Vibrant colors in your foyer, photos of children laughing, or funky artwork will work too!

Fire Is Passion and Drama

Bring the Fire Element in by incorporating a sense of drama to your home through your choice of color and artwork. One client of mine, clearly possessing a sufficient amount of Fire in her personality, has a warm home filled with bright reds, oranges, and blues and artwork with people from her native home of Cuba. It is such a fun and welcoming space, reflecting her warm and welcoming personality!

Fire Lights Others Up

We crave light. It's essential for well-being. It has a great impact not only on our moods and emotions, but also on our behavior. In the northern countries seasonal affective disorder (SAD) is a type of depression brought on by the lack of natural light in winter. It disrupts our circadian cycles, which inhibits the production of serotonin and lowers mood. Leverage the sunlight in your home. Especially if you work from home, find ways to use the rooms so that you can take advantage of the sun throughout the day. Create a few comfortable mobile office spaces with access to the sun and nature views.

If possible, take a break during your day and go for a walk or just sit outside. Access to sunlight improves our mood.

THE FIRE ELEMENT IN THE GARDEN

There are many ways to incorporate Fire into our outdoor areas. It's become rather trendy to have a fire pit in the yard, which evokes the memories of campfires and bonfires on the beach with a group of good friends. Even pretty, delicately strung lights and candles around the seating area provide a sense of connection.

Gardens benefit from touches of red, orange, purple, or pink flowers to give a punch of bold color. Put out some patio furniture in Fire fabric colors. Star, pyramid, and triangular shapes represent Fire. Adding a Japanese pagoda statue or stringing stars along a fence represents Fire. Also, statues of animals such as a rooster or horse symbolize Fire. Even red brick masonry will pull in the Fire Element.

THE FIRE ELEMENT IN NATURE

When was the last time that you consciously watched the sunset? I ask this question during workshops, and it's amazing to hear the majority of people last saw one on vacation when they made it a special event. Breaking news: the sun sets *every* day. Make it a point to notice it on the way home from work or gazing out your window. You don't need to spend an hour watching it. Here is a challenge: For the next week, stop what you are doing for a few minutes and notice the sunset. See the gorgeous colors turn from pale to deep and brilliant. Perhaps you'll catch the "golden hour." Learn to appreciate this daily gift of life.

Or watch the sunrise. I am not an early riser so this is a challenge for me; however, every so often I decide it's time to set that clock, drive to the beach, and watch the sun come up. It truly is a magical time of day, still and quiet, with the gentle calls of the morning birds and the feeling of promise of a new day. You can understand how indigenous cultures revered the sun.

Fire is the peak of the sun, so noontime is a great way to connect and notice the sun, and the summer solstice is the peak of the annual sun cycle. Acknowledging these sacred patterns in our lives brings us closer to the Fire Element.

I connect with Fire on a daily basis, not just by going out into the sun for a walk or to sit, but by acknowledging its warmth and light. Doing this consciously is so much more powerful than not. Perhaps sit at a campfire or light your outdoor fire pit and enjoy this evening with some friends. Or for a more contemplative moment light a candle and watch the flames as you breathe and perhaps meditate.

THE SACRED

FIRE MEDITATION

Light a candle and sit on the edge of a cushion, pillow, or blanket. Sit with your hands comfortably in your lap. Close your eyes and notice the rise and fall of your breath. Take your time during this visualization, calling up as much detail as possible.

Imagine that you are surrounded by golden white light from the heavens. Without any pain, observe this white-hot light coming down to your crown chakra and burning the top of your head as it works its way slowly down your body burning away all the negativity, all the bad experiences, all karma from the past, present, and future. Let it burn away all that no longer serves you—memories and trauma, unkind words and deeds, judgment and carelessness.

As it reaches your feet, see your entire body in flames. Your skeleton becomes strong, hard, and resilient as the flames move down into your feet.

In the shell of who you were there is strength, resilience, and power. You step onto a soft, white lotus blossom and feel the coolness on the soles of your feet. The blossom grows up your feet creating beautiful new skin. See it rise up your body, forming new skin and organs, muscles and tendons. You now have a new heart and new lungs, renewed chakras. See a beautiful point of light glowing in your heart and watch it expand to encompass your entire body.

Send loving kindness out to your circle of close family and friends and feel their loving kindness come back to you. Then send out loving kindness to a wider circle of family, friends, colleagues. And receive their loving kindness back. Send loving kindness out to all sentient beings, including Mother Earth, all the trees, flowers, plants, mountains, wildlife, rocks, the planets, and stars. And feel their loving kindness come back to you.

Make a wish and hold it in your heart. Slowly open your eyes.

Feel what has been stirred within you. Feel that flame within your heart.

—Adaptation of the Heart Sutra meditation
from the teachings of H. H. Grandmaster Professor Lin Yun

CASE STUDIES

Barbara Was Burnt Out

Barbara is a vibrant young woman with a brilliant smile and a heart to match—sure signs of the Fire Element. However, when I first met her, there was a great sadness within her, like her fire had nearly gone out. Her heart was broken in her current marriage, and she felt "used."

She told me that she had been so distraught one evening that she collapsed with grief while her son sat steps away in the family room. When she made several dramatic attempts to get his attention and there was no response from him, her grief became all the more unbearable.

This is a clear sign of Fire out of balance. Fire cannot be ignored. And when Fire doesn't get the support and nurturing she craves, she feels empty and hopeless. Her Fire goes out.

While walking through Barbara's home, we discussed how she used each room. She shared with me that she had moved out of the master bedroom because she was estranged from her husband, preferring to sleep in the family room on the couch. Anyone who has slept on a couch for even one night would see how it would be challenging to fully rest and restore herself night after night.

Touring the master bedroom, it was clear that there was an abundance of the Metal Element. There was a prevalence of the colors of white and gray, as well as chrome and metal furnishings. This naturally made Barbara feel very uncomfortable on a subconscious level. The Fire Element is the Grandparent to Metal and therefore controls Metal, but in the process its energy can be greatly exhausted. That is how she described sleeping there. She couldn't rest.

She preferred to sleep in the family room because it felt so cozy! The family room had wood paneling (the Wood Element) and there was a beautiful fireplace that was lit all winter long. The room was filled with leather and red (both Fire Element symbols). This space truly nourished her Fire spirit and was helping her get through this extremely emotional period in her life.

My suggestion to her was to convert a beautiful unused guest room into a sanctuary. I suggested that she add both Wood and Fire Elements to it to support her. For the Wood Element, she brought in several plants and artwork with flowers. For Fire, she painted a bright coral color to an accent wall and laid out bed linens in the same hue. She also added some Earth—a great stabilizing Element—with some beiges and browns to complement the coral. As I suggested, she started a meditation practice immediately and deepened her studies on spirituality.

I saw Barbara recently, and her eyes told me that the Fire spirit was alive and well in her. She lit up the room! She was in the process of a divorce and was finally moving forward in her career with determination. She had found a great sanctuary in her new bedroom, which she moved into the night after our consultation. She has a regular meditation practice and has become calm and grounded, while wrapping her arms around all she meets. She is an inspiration, just like Fire!

Mary's Heart Opener

Mary called me to help her transition during a divorce from her husband of nearly twenty years. Although she had initiated the divorce, her life was unsettled by all the changes that were happening very fast.

Mary was very successful in her corporate role. She managed a team of ten employees and handled many complex projects simultaneously. Her organization and leadership skills were well suited to the task. She had confidence and ambition and earned a good salary with generous bonuses—a testament to her work ethic.

Her True Nature Element was Metal, but upon our discussing her challenges, I found that she was deficient in both Fire and Earth. She was a wonderful, supportive mother, but had several challenges in relationships. Her heart felt rather closed when we discussed that area of her life.

Although things were going smoothly on the legal front (it was an amicable divorce), she found that she was navigating treacherous waters of emotional bereavement. Upon reflection, she realized that it was partially because her parents had divorced while she was young and she still felt the pain of that event in her life. She found that although she thought she had moved beyond it, her grieving had been resurrected with the failing of her own marriage. In addition, it was painful for her to think of her own experience of having to "grow up" at too young an age in caring for her sister and the responsibility that she had assumed, and she didn't want that for her children.

It was clear in our discussion about relationships that Mary was guarded. She said that she was unable to truly love and accept herself. She had great strength as a mother and in her work life, but in relationships that required vulnerability, such as romantic attachments and friendships, her heart was closed. She lacked a supportive network of close friends. She felt unsuccessful in this area of her life, and that was uncomfortable to admit. In my work, these are signs of weakened Fire and Earth Elements.

When she spoke about her work relationships and specific situations, she seemed very direct and perhaps a bit punitive with others. This is often what those with overactive Metal do to protect themselves from feeling vulnerable.

Sometimes my clients already know what they need. Mary told me that she had considered getting a dog for her children to help with the transition. Pets represent the Fire Element, and what better way to open the heart than through the unconditional love a pet can give! I urged her to follow her intuition.

Among the recommendations that we discussed, I asked her to connect with the Fire and Earth Elements in nature and in her home. She added Fire with some candles and touches of red to her bedroom. She also put up images of intimate couples in her bedroom (also Fire). I suggested that she connect to the sun often during her workday (she had a good view from her office window). She painted her bedroom a soft yellow and placed a few rose quartz crystals (the "love" crystals) on her nightstand—both Earth Element symbols—which aid her in connecting with her heart chakra.

I also asked Mary to start paying attention to her dreams and to journal. This process could help her open up to the past and issues that needed to be processed and dealt with. (Metal represents the emotion of grief.) Also, Metal personalities tend to see themselves as the authority and leader and often need to experience for themselves firsthand what their higher selves are saying to them. And when you decide to open that connection to your higher self, you better believe that it responds!

To drain the excess Metal in her personality, I suggested that she purchase a water fountain for her foyer or, at the very least, a beautiful painting of the ocean with waves heading into the home—the waves represent chi entering the home.

As with most consultations, we did a space clearing and blessing on her home to remove any negativity from the past and infuse it with possibilities for the present and future. While I channeled divine spirit and repeated the mantras of a special ceremonial clearing and blessing, Mary's Metal helped me "hold the space" while envisioning all the negativity gathering up and dispersing from the house. After I finished the prayers, she told me that she "saw" the energy as black smoke that gathered into the center of the home and rose up and out of the chimney into the sky. It was a greatly refreshing and invigorating experience for the both of us!

IGNITE YOUR FIRE POWER!

Too much Fire in our personalities will show up as a chaotic and frantic life. Unable to focus, we move from one activity to another. There may be a fear of being alone, which we falsely translate as "lonely." When Fire burns too hot and too long, it will burn out. This collapsed Fire leads to a lack of energy and passion for life. We may also feel isolated and sad or even depressed, confused, and anxious. Clients with low or collapsed Fire typically tell me they feel disconnected from others and lack joy in their lives. They do not accept themselves or others for who they are. They can be either overly judgmental or too tolerant of bad behavior.

Balanced Fire is energetic, loving, and passionate. Fire is a great connector with people. Fire people light up the room when they enter and have abundant energy to give to everyone. Fire is the performer, be it on a stage, at a business meeting, or as a charismatic speaker in general. Fire people wow us with their intensity! We all benefit from their joie de vivre.

If this sounds like you, reclaim your Fire power! Ignite your Fire with the suggestions in this chapter. Bring the Fire Element into your home. Get a pet or actually *play* with your pet!

Wear the Fire Element to help you embody the qualities of the Wizard. You can activate Fire by wearing clothes that are sexy, dramatic, or attention-getting, such as animal print, leather, and suede fabrics, as well as in the colors of Fire (red, orangey red, pink, and purple). It is very easy to spot Fire people: they are usually the ones in red and leopard prints with lots of large jewelry pieces—and perhaps even a crown!

Add the Fire Element to your bedroom and special space. Sit by a Fire and be conscious of its energy. Watch the sunrise. Be more expansive and open your heart. Let others in. We all need the warmth and connection that Fire brings into our lives!

Chapter 7

The Earth Element

There are a thousand ways to kneel and kiss the earth.

—Rumi

What have we learned about the Earth Element, so far? Earth represents security and stability, the ability to feel grounded and balanced. It provides us nourishment and support.

The Earth Element represents the energy of late summer and late afternoon moving past the peak brilliance of Fire. Earth is known as the transitional element placed at critical junctures of the Five Element Cycle—traditionally following Fire or summer, the peak of yang chi. Earth provides a stabilizing factor that allows transformation to take place.

The Earth is our home and provides nourishment for all beings on it. It represents the ripening of the fruits that blossomed in the summer and are now ready to harvest. It is sweetness and the joy of togetherness.

Earth is the abundant soil and sand, from rock that makes up its surface through millions of years of compression, heat, and erosion. Sedimentary rock represents the layers of erosion from wind and water. Metamorphic rock represents the processes of compression. And igneous rock from volcanic eruptions represents the force of heat.

Earth is the horizontal surface, the stable base we can rely on. Earth grounds us and gives us constancy. The quality of the soil must be in balance. If too porous (weak) or too dense (packed), little life can be sustained by it. Earth nourishes life and provides a safe haven. It is the sacred ground we walk upon and completes the Cosmic Trinity of Heaven—Humanity—Earth.

Walk through the grass; enjoy the warm sand on your feet. The energy we get from that direct connection to the earth is life-affirming. It is said that the earth resonates at the same hertz as the human brain (roughly 7–8 Hz), and this direct connection is actually vital to our health.

Earth is the ash created and nourished by the Fire Element. It is controlled, or dispersed, by the sprouting of organic matter, the Wood Element; and its chi is drained and transmuted into the metals and minerals of the earth, which is the Metal Element.

Do any of the words describing Earth speak to you?

THE MIDDLE WAY

In biophilic terms, the Earth Element is all about proper balance and placement within the space. It is associated with all the features of the earth, great and small, from the mountain ranges and deserts to pebbles and grains of sand.

Because of its inherent stability, the Earth Element embodies the energy of the Middle Way or Eightfold Path in Buddhism. To reach liberation from suffering, one lives in accordance with this path: right view, right intention, right speech, right action, right effort, right livelihood, right mindfulness, and right concentration. Following this path is to avoid the extremes of life, to strive for balance and harmony, and to hopefully to achieve enlightenment.

Nature inherently has great diversity and always strives for balance between yin and yang. These qualities are vital to sustain healthy ecosystems, as well as to allow for change and adaptation.

Because of this, we have an abundance of species and varieties within each species. There are an estimated 1,500–2,500 species of orchid alone!

The horror of the mid-1800s Great Famine in Ireland was largely due to a lack of diversity. Farmers gravitated to planting the "Irish Lumper," a specific potato variety easy to cultivate. For a time, potatoes were in abundance and fed a growing population that depended on this single crop for survival. But when the environment changed and a disease swept this specific crop, the Irish were devastated.

Variability and diversity are part of the natural world, and how we have experienced the world throughout our evolution. Look out your window right now and notice the abundant varieties of green in just this small view. It's spring as I write this, and I see such a world of greens from the newly budded lime-green leaves to the brilliant greens of the grass to the dark greens of the evergreen foliage. Notice the different shapes and sizes of each plant and tree. Imagine that you only had a view of maple trees or just yellow tulips. How boring and stagnant that would be! Variety creates a feeling of vitality and abundance. It creates a dynamic landscape.

The relationship of yin and yang demonstrates this variety inherent in nature: light and shade, hard and soft, rounded and spiky, tall and short. These are all ways to describe the abundance of variety in our spaces. Applied to our own environments—your home, specifically—take a look at the room you are currently in. Notice the abundance (or not) of diversity and variety in this space.

Although the possibilities are endless, below are some examples of how you can contrast yin-yang:

- A round table with square-edged furnishings
- The softness of upholstered chairs paired with the hardness of a metal table
- Dark walls with light trim and ceiling

- Wood floors with an area rug
- A large window with soft window treatments
- Angular quartz crystals and soft, lacy pillows

If a room feels good, it probably has a good mixture of yin and yang elements in it. Usually if a room feels out of balance, it is because there is too much yin (too quiet and stagnant) or too much yang (too loud and busy).

- If there is too much yin in a space, it will contribute to a feeling of lethargy and a lack of vitality. It can make you feel lazy and unwilling to try new things, for that will require leaving the safety and security of this space. Too much yin can lead to sadness, illness, and depression.
- If there is too much yang in a space, it contributes to very high energy and stress. There is no space to relax and breathe. You move from one project to another at a quick pace without pausing to reflect on the most efficient way to tackle it or even the merit of doing that task. Too much yang can lead to being burnt out and illness, anxiety and high blood pressure.

But just know that feng shui provides us with tools, not rules. We need to be flexible when applying them. For instance, some people have extremely stressful jobs and work environments, such as in a hospital or on a police beat. Their home should be more yin to help establish more balance in their lives and allow them greater opportunity to decompress—perhaps a canopy bed with soft lighting and curves in the bedroom. Others may work in extremely yin environments, such as a mortuary. They could use more yang chi in their homes to provide more vitality and energy—perhaps brighter lighting and colorful rooms.

Feng shui is known as the art of placement, and placement plays a key role in feng shui as well as biophilic design. Mindful placement means that the selection and positioning of furnishings and objects were done with awareness and consciousness, that some considered thought went into the decoration of your home.

One of the most important aspects of mindful placement is the balance of "prospect and refuge." This concept arises from our primitive times in a savanna-type landscape. "Prospect" refers to the ability to scan the horizon for both food sources and any threat to survival. "Refuge" refers to a place that provides protection and security from those threats.

Prospect and refuge therefore require an open view of the space that is sufficiently lit so that you see what may be approaching as well as a canopy of protection at your back, including solid walls and perhaps a lowered ceiling or screening around that position.

Prospect and refuge are said to trigger the parasympathetic system or relaxation response—the opposite of the fight-or-flight response we are all too familiar with. It is best to have prospect and refuge anyplace where you spend a considerable amount of time including your bed and work desk.

This concept is extremely intuitive in certain situations. Imagine that you are being brought to a table at a restaurant and given the option of two chairs. You might select the chair that will give you a full view of the room. This is the most comfortable position to be in. However, you may give this chair to your companion in deference to their need for comfort. Notice this next time you are out.

In feng shui, we call this the "command position" or "power position." And we recognize this as an extremely significant environmental factor that will contribute to greater or poorer health, especially with the placement of our bed and desk.

EARTH ARCHETYPE: THE PEACEMAKER

The Earth Element's archetype is The Peacemaker, seeking harmony in the world. It is about the ability to trust and accept love and support from others. It allows you to acknowledge your right to be fully alive and to engage in happiness and love. These are all qualities of balanced Earth.

Earth Is Nourishment

Earth provides all the nurturing qualities of the Mother archetype. Although the Mother seems to denote only feminine qualities, men can equally personify this archetype. Family and home are the utmost concerns, where the Earth person anticipates the needs and cares of others. Many Earth people prefer to stay at home to care for the family. Often, the sole purpose of work is to earn the ability to provide for the family. Earth gives nourishment for all. The kitchen is the center of activity. Earth is fruitful, empathetic, and resilient and provides healing and forgiveness.

. . . Or the Out-of-Balance Mother

However, when the Earth Element is out of balance, she is plagued by worry and tends to sacrifice of herself for others; she is unable to set appropriate boundaries in her personal relationships. She extends herself to the point of collapse. An appropriate balance of Earth is recognizing the need to take care of yourself first and to give to others from the spillover. Just like the safety announcement on airlines, put the mask on yourself first and then you can help others. Imbalanced Earth may need to learn that taking care of yourself isn't being selfish; it's mandatory!

As a strong Fire and Wood type, career is extremely important to my friend Lynn. Juggling a family during her career ascension was a challenge. Now working as an entrepreneur, she continually learns that wanting to be everything to everyone can result in burnout, worry, and great self-sacrifice. Needing to please many competing groups as well as family has proven to be a sign of our modern times. Guilt and worry can be constant companions until we find ways to nurture ourselves and come back to center.

Earth Is Grounded and Stable

Earth is the ground we walk upon—always there, always available. She is about responsibility and follow-through. She prefers to work behind the scenes, keeping everything moving along. She is trustworthy and practical and prefers to be a team player.

Being grounded is one of Lynn's skills. While working in a group on an extremely stressful and tense project, one of her colleagues turned to her and said that she really loved the feeling of calmness and peace Lynn brought to the project. Lynn was so taken aback because internally she said that she certainly did *not* feel calm and peaceful! That's the power of our energy.

. . . Or Stuck and Averse to Change

Stability sometimes leads to stuckness. Earth can become fearful of change and lost in the past, unable to live in the present. She may become overly sentimental, surrounding herself with family memorabilia. Earth can sometimes stay in the same home that they grew up in, or if they must, at least stay in a home for many decades. Earth often stays in jobs and romantic relationships due to a feeling of loyalty and, of course, fear of change.

A cousin of mine is always reminiscing about the past to the point that he doesn't live in the moment or for the future. He eats the same meals and does his chores the same days, week after week, year after year. This is imbalanced Earth to an extreme. There is no room for growth and expansion.

Earth Is Proper Boundaries and Support

Earth sees the importance of self-sacrifice for the greater good. She has the capacity to see both sides and is generous in nature. However, she sets proper boundaries. The Mother knows how much to give and how much to withhold. She understands that others need to learn their lessons and she is not an enabler that will keep others bound to her. She provides unconditional love and support, but acknowledges and respects her own needs, desires, and path.

. . . Or Overextended and Self-Pitying

Because Earth is seemingly always available, others may take advantage of her and not return her need to feel nurtured and loved. She has difficulty saying no. Her great desire to be needed at all costs may overshadow her self-respect.

On the other hand, she often has difficulty accepting love and support from others. She hides behind a cheerful front and appears self-sufficient. She tends to set unrealistic expectations in relationships and often ends up in disappointment. When exaggerated, she may collapse into self-pity and martyrdom. This state only exacerbates her belief that she has no support or love. She distrusts people, and because she is no fun to have around when in this state, she is often left out.

One of Lynn's great parental lessons in life—and perhaps one you experience too—was to know how much to give and how much to pull back. With both of her children she saw the results of being overinvolved in their lives, and it wasn't pretty. But her fear was that if she pulled back, she would be viewed as a "bad mother," selfish or lacking care. Once Lynn realized and was aware of her meddling, she had to care *less* about what others thought of her behavior. Again, it was important to come back into balance.

Earth Is the Center

Desiring harmony above all, Earth maintains the center in all relationships. She is a great negotiator, seeing both sides. She strives for a win-win outcome for all. She is diplomatic and knows how to work a room! Just like the archetype of the Mother, she connects with people and truly hears them. She is trustworthy and trusting of others. Her empathetic and peaceful presence is a great asset to any group.

When Lynn first started working in the technology sector, she quickly learned the power of the Peacemaker. She was an account manager who had multiple parties to please. On one hand she had her clients, who were often obstinate and unreasonable. On the other hand, she had the internal staff who were overworked and stressed, but she needed them to do her work quickly and efficiently. She learned the power of Earth: connection, listening, and negotiating to get what she needed and when she needed it. It was a valuable lesson that has served her well ever since.

The archetype of the Peacemaker throughout history has been the Mother and all beings that have put others first in their lives. They are the caretakers, health care professionals, teachers, advocates, and those dedicated to organizations at the service of others.

Earth types have several of these features: a generous mouth and full lips, a rounded face, a broad bridge of the nose, puffy upper eyelids. They tend to have a roundness to their bodies, large breasts or muscles, and a yellowish tone to their skin (regardless of race).

Too little Earth can result in swollen glands, weak ankles and wrists, varicose veins, easy bruising, and the inability to feel full. Too much Earth can lead to an excessive appetite, water retention, heavy eyes and head, and puffy eyelids.

In an Earth person's home, the kitchen is where the life is. You cannot visit without being fixed a snack or a meal. Cabinets and closets are stuffed to capacity, perhaps overcompensating for fear of feeling empty inside. Oftentimes, everything is everywhere in her house. She can have a lot of clutter, but to her these items are precious, often sentimental. She has a story for everything and why she needs to keep it.

Strengths and Weaknesses

Strengths—Responsible, reliable, grounded, stable, patient, committed to goals, sympathetic, poised, attentive, good at assembling others to a task, being of service to others, good at negotiation, mediates conflict, gives/receives support from others, talented at achieving the most cooperation with the least sacrifice, creates environment of trust.

Weaknesses—Can get stuck (mud), not comfortable in a leadership role, averse to/often ignores conflict, insecurity, does not like change, meddlesome, worried, conforming, scattered, wishy-washy, prone to too much self-sacrifice, dependent, can be unrealistic, can have issues around personal boundaries, victim mentality, smothering, low self-esteem, martyr syndrome, enables codependent relationships, unable to accept love and/or help.

Earth is nourished by the Fire Element. Wood's forceful upward movement balances Earth's tendency to harden and solidify. So Earth is controlled by the Wood Element. For instance, the natural driving impulse of Wood disrupts Earth's tendency to remain still. As Earth (soil) compacts and consolidates over millions of years, it forms veins of natural minerals (Metal), therefore Earth's chi is drained by Metal. Earth forms boundaries, earthen banks, that channel the flow of Water, therefore Earth controls Water.

In our lives, Earth represents the Earth Mother. It symbolizes nurturing and protection and the intimate bonds in our lives, including romantic relationships. And because healthy relationships require inner work and balance, Earth also symbolizes contemplation and constancy. Earth is identified with the center of a space due to its stabilizing character.

THE EARTH ELEMENT IN THE HOME

The Earth Element is at its most essential, powerful nature when we connect with what is beneath our feet: soil, rocks, quartz, granite, marble, and crystals. The more raw and primitive the stone is, the greater its Earth essence and impact. I collect beach rocks and love displaying them in bowls around my home.

We recognize the power of Earth with exposed brick walls in old buildings. Old brick has great essence and patina acquired with age. Granite counters and stone flooring are other great ways to tap into the stability of Earth. Materials also made from the soil are ceramic, terracotta, clay, and tile. Earth is symbolized through the coziness of chenille, velvet, and flannel fabrics.

The colors of Earth are the hues of the soil from sandy beige to peat moss brown, as well as orangey clays, yellow, and peach. Earth is a great neutral color that provides a wonderful foundation to showcase other colors and objects. Its hues are great for creating calm, grounded spaces.

The shapes of the Earth Element are those associated with the horizon: a flat surface as well as square shapes. Contemporary furnishings with their low horizontal lines are a great way to bring in the energy of Earth.

Artwork that symbolizes Earth includes mountains or open landscapes. A beautiful mountain scene can help you feel more solid, strong, and stable.

Earth Is Nourishment

The kitchen is the place of the quintessential Earth type. This is where you dish out nourishment and acceptance. Be sure that your kitchen is tidy and clean. Use all the burners on your stove to activate the "health and wealth" that your stove represents.

The refrigerator is often overlooked when decluttering. Go through your refrigerator and check labels and clear out all old food. Wash the interior and reorganize. This will allow for good, healthy chi to circulate for your food.

Be aware of your energy while you cook. Are you feeling rushed, put-upon, and perhaps even resentful? That energy is being transmitted into the food you prepare and consume. Also be aware of the energy of *what* you cook. Fresh, organic produce and consciously-raised meats have much greater positive chi than commercial processed food.

Earth Is Grounded and Stable

Just as the soil of the earth beneath our feet provides stability, the floors in our homes provide the solid base we require in our lives. We need to be mindful of the quality of the floors in our home. Floors are a metaphor for honoring the ground you walk upon, your path, and the respect you have for others and yourself. Are there creaks in the wood, broken tiles, or old carpeting well beyond its years?

Earth Is Proper Boundaries

Check the boundaries in your home and property. Do you have defined boundaries between you and your neighbors? Do you have boundaries between grass, untamed vegetation, and a garden?

How about the boundaries between ceilings and walls? Is there a clear line between the two? Consider any molding that may need repair or maintenance.

Open floor plans are the rule in modern homes. Is there a clear boundary to separate spaces in these rooms, such as furnishings, area rugs, or lighting? You can establish some boundaries using tall cabinets, bookcases, or even moving furnishings to create the illusion of one. If you share your bedroom or home office with a partner, are there boundaries for personal space?

Earth Is the Center

The Earth Element represents the center of the home. This space is the focus of the energy inside it. Consider it the seed point of energy from which our homes blossomed and thrive.

What is going on in the center of your home? Is it a closet or other storage space? If so, are these spaces neat and tidy or cluttered and sloppy? Is there a bathroom? Be sure that this room is clean and well-maintained. Any leaks must be repaired—the metaphor is that any leaks will drain our energy.

Is there a stairway? Be sure it is safe, that there is no clutter and the stairs are lit well. Is there a hallway? Be sure that the hallway is uncluttered and allows chi to move. To the best of your ability, be sure that the center of your home is open and gives chi room to circulate and breathe.

THE EARTH ELEMENT IN THE GARDEN

In our outdoor spaces, rock gardens are one of my personal favorites for connecting with the Earth Element. Large boulders can be turned into focal points, and they can often be used to resolve another feng shui challenge on the land, such as a sloping yard. The boulder provides stability where the landform is weakened. Stone provides a wonderful juxtaposition with green plants for the balance of yin and yang.

Stone benches and seating are good ways to connect with Earth. Using stone that is local to your area is a great way to welcome and invite the spirit of place onto your property. And the patina of stone as it oxidizes . . . gives the stone presence.

Paths to our doors or garden space can be made with stone, such as bluestone or rough pieces of slate. I often suggest putting in a simple stone path from the road to their door to suburban clients, who typically have one path to the door from the driveway to enhance the wonderful energy (which translates as opportunities in feng shui) from their neighborhood. Pebble pathways activate the sense of hearing (the crunch of the pebbles under foot) and slow down our physical bodies (did you ever try to walk quickly on pebbles?).

New England has an abundance of stone in the land, and I love driving through some of the old towns to see their beautiful stone walls, many of them built over one to two hundred years ago separating properties. I live on Long Island, which is not much more than sandy soil with an occasional rock outcrop only on the northernmost shoreline.

I admire properties with a glacial erratic on the lawn. These are large lone boulders that were deposited by the ice age millions of years ago. They have stood their ground all that time. And what great power they possess!

It is often a good idea to have proper boundaries between your neighbors' land and yours. Install fencing or landscaping. Check the condition of your boundaries. Stone edging and retaining walls are a great natural addition to the garden.

Check the boundaries between gardens and natural landscaping. If one spills into the other, create definition with a small stacked stone wall or dig a shallow narrow trench in the soil to delineate the spaces.

The most common material for Earth is the soil. In ancient times, feng shui masters would spend quite a bit of time evaluating the quality of the soil in different locations before they provided a good location to build. Soil can be sandy, it can be dense with roots and stones, or it can be loamy peat moss that is so rich and full of nutrients it will allow any plant to grow to its full potential.

THE EARTH ELEMENT IN NATURE

Dig in the earth, smell the soil, and feel it in your hands. Research has shown that when we come into contact with certain bacteria in soil, the serotonin in our bodies is activated, which elevates mood and decreases anxiety.

I love to lie on the sand when I'm at the beach. The warmth of the sand is comforting. Next time you have the opportunity, feel where the earth touches your body and let your body melt into the earth. Feel the earth as it supports you completely.

Take a hike through a wooded area and breathe in the scents of the ground beneath you. The air smells different—so fresh and energizing. Notice how the earth feels on your feet. Is it hard-packed earth or soft and giving to the impact of your gait?

Climb a mountain. At the summit, observe the yin and yang of the mountains in view—the valleys, dips, and peaks. Feel the mountain's strength beneath your feet. This is known as Dragon Chi. The Chinese saw animal forms in all natural creations. In walking the mountains the Chinese say that you "chase the dragon." Can you see the Dragon's movement among the mountains before you?

While on a walk, look for stones that stand out or seem to call to you. Collect some and place them in a bowl in your home. Hold these stones and feel the energy of your local community and the land. These stones have been there for a long time absorbing the qualities from that particular place.

Find a large boulder in the sun and lay down, feeling your body connect with the warmth and power of the Earth. This is especially nice to do alongside a stream, hearing the calming sound of the water.

Notice the time of day associated with Earth—late afternoon hours—and sense the quality of light and energy. Do you seem to slow down, have a lull, or are you energized and full of activity?

The grounding energies of the Earth provide our bodies with necessary nutrients, just as the sun provides warmth and vitamin D. We cannot see this energy, but many who are sensitive enough can detect it. They may get a tingling sensation. For others, it's a feel-good sensation that you can't quite put your finger on while enjoying the outdoors.

For millions of years, our species has walked the Earth. We've lived amid and with nature. Our intelligence has come through our senses and observation. But now we are completely severed from this primitive relationship with the Earth. We are surrounded by reprocessed air, synthetic materials, and by electromagnetic fields from all the wireless technology, appliances, and cell phones. The combination of these effects is more than the parts. They work together to create a techno-chemical soup, which puts stress on our bodies and often manifests as physical exhaustion, illness, and emotional and spiritual stress.

In addition, rubber-soled or plastic shoes have replaced leather-soled shoes for many of us. What effect does this have on our bodies? It insulates us from absorbing the natural electric charge from the Earth, just as rubber tires on our cars protect us from lightning.

Walk barefoot on the earth. This is also known as Earthing, a growing movement that acknowledges the Earth's natural energy and its link to health. Remember, the earth resonates at the same hertz as our brains, and this direct connection is actually vital to our health.

Walk barefoot on grass, dirt, or the beach. In order to benefit from these energies, you need direct contact with the earth (not concrete, tile, or even wood floors).

You can also sleep on the Earth, as we've done for millions of years. But even sleeping in a sleeping bag will not do. You must have some part of your skin in contact with the Earth to be grounded.

THE SACRED

OBSERVING THE ENERGY OF THE LAND

We live in a world of ordinary as well as nonordinary reality. Shamans from all of the world's cultures know this to be a fact and are able to travel between these states of reality. Our ordinary reality is often obscured by our chattering minds. If you want to observe the nonordinary, try this exercise:

Go to a place in nature that feels good to you. It's most important that you can be alone here and not distracted by the presence of other people, unless, of course, they are willing to do this exercise with you.

Sit in a comfortable spot and center yourself by being mindful of your inhale and exhale. You can close your eyes at first. But then, slowly open your eyes and scan over the land to see where your attention is drawn. Stop anywhere you feel attracted to and stare at the air just above the object. Stare long enough for your eyes to become unfocused and slightly blurry. Try not to blink, but if you do, just bring yourself back to the unfocused stare.

Be very open and aware. You may notice movement in the area around where you are placing your attention. You may see its energy field or something else. I often see the energy field as a whitish color that hovers and sometimes slowly rises upward. This exercise works whether you are focusing on a mountain range or on a flower. Feel the connection and give gratitude.

Dowsing

Within and around the Earth are a variety of lines of energy and cosmic forces. Some of these lines are part of the electromagnetic field that encircles the Earth. Others are part of the geographic features within the Earth itself, such as water courses, fault lines, and various types of rock strata.

The ancient practice of dowsing is one way to connect to these invisible Earth energies. One of the more popular tools is divining rods, also called L-rods due to their shape. Pendulums are also used.

For centuries, perhaps millennia, dowsers were called upon to locate underground water streams for wells in villages and for farming. They would look for sites where the water was closest to the surface and had the best quality and quantity for people's needs.

Learning the practice of dowsing has been a very sacred way for me to connect and communicate with Mother Earth and to discover what is ordinarily hidden—the secrets below and around us.

Although these energy lines are neither good nor bad, water is the best absorber of energy so it easily "picks up" the energy from human activity, for better or worse. Once these streams pick up negative energy, they will transmit it into the land and impact the health and well-being of those living above it.

I use dowsing to assist clients in finding these negative energy lines and neutralizing their impact for improved health of the land, the wildlife, vegetation, and people.

DOWSING EXERCISE

This is the workshop exercise that I mentioned in the beginning of chapter 2. And you can learn to do it yourself!

You'll need a wire hanger (not the kind with cardboard tube), wire clippers, a straw, and a willing participant.

Clip the hanger along the long side in the middle and then clip the wire on both sides of the curved part to remove it. You'll now have two sections of the hanger. Bend them so that they are shaped like an L. Cut the straw in half and place these on the smaller sides of the Ls. These will be your handles. You now have a pair of dowsing rods!

Stand and hold the rods with the straw end about waist high. Make sure that the long end is roughly parallel to the ground and pointing out in front of you. It may take a while for the rods to stop rotating. They are responding to your energy! Just breathe and they will settle down.

Have your friend stand about eight feet in front of you. Slowly walk towards them and ask for the rods to spread open when you reach the edge of their energy field (left rod to the left and right rod to the right). Note the distance between the rods and your friend. This is where their energy field begins. It might be two to four feet away from their body.

If you want to continue the fun, ask your friend to think of something that makes them angry or frustrated (yes, this will be fun!) and repeat the exercise. You will probably notice that their energy field contracts: you are able to get closer to them before the rods finally open. Then, walk back to your starting point and ask your friend to think of something fabulous! Their energy field should expand.

So what is going on? The dowsing rods are actually responding to the energy emanating from their heart chakra. When we have negative feelings such as anger, guilt, shame, or sadness, our heart chakra closes up. But when we have positive feelings, our heart chakras expand.

You can learn to use your dowsing rods to ask all sorts of magical questions, including the location of negative or positive energy in the earth.

QUARTZ CRYSTAL MEDITATION

Any crystal can be used for meditation, but I recommend quartz crystal because it is readily available. It facilitates wisdom, clarity of thought, and higher consciousness and fosters communication between the conscious mind and the subconscious, activating all levels of consciousness. However, please feel free to use a crystal that you feel drawn to and have an energetic connection with.

First, it is important to know that you should clear your crystal when you take it home. If you have a crystal already and you haven't cleared it, take the time to do that now.

There are many clearing methods you can use, but here are two that I've employed. You can simply place your crystal out in the bright sun or full moon. Or you can immerse your crystal in a bowl of course sea salt and leave it there overnight.

When you are ready, sit in a quiet place and hold the crystal in both hands, or lie down and place it on your solar plexus just above the navel. Be aware of your inhale and exhale. Take a slow deep breath in, and as you let it out, feel any tension in your body just drain away.

Breathe and shift the focus of your attention to the crystal you are holding.

Feel the energy of the stone. Imagine that you are becoming one with this energy and synchronize with its vibration.

Notice any changes anywhere in your body, and then let them go.

Stay in this visualization space until you feel that you are finished. It could be two minutes or it could be ten or more. Give gratitude to the crystal for its help and to the Great Divine Spirit for what you have experienced. Now, you can place this stone on your altar or another place where you can see it daily. Remember, you can do this meditation with any stone.

CASE STUDIES

Clara and the Falling-Apart House

Clara is a beautiful, warm person with a playful, funky side. She has purple hair, a fun, outgoing personality, and lots of fun, eclectic artwork in her home. Her primary Element is Fire.

She shared her house with a partner who did construction for a living. And one of her great challenges was echoed in that old proverb that "the shoemaker's children go barefoot." There were several rooms in her house that were in complete disarray, obviously in the middle of renovation. In fact, her bedroom did not have interior walls on three sides, and the insulation was exposed. The air quality in the house was so poor that she had developed terrible allergies and asthma and suffered from chronic bronchitis.

The only room that was completely renovated and functioned well was the kitchen, where she and her partner loved to cook. In our discussion Clara admitted that she was not happy in this relationship. And I discovered that she had another house that she rented out. All the walls were intact there, and it was a good shape. I pointed out the obvious, which is what I often do: I suggested that she move into the other house while she reconsidered this relationship.

The falling-apart house was a metaphor for her relationship with her partner and herself. She was not honoring her needs and, therefore, was in a dead-end relationship. This was a clear imbalance in the Earth Element. She was afraid to rock the boat with her partner and draw clear boundaries on what was acceptable and what was not. So, in return, she felt disappointed and sacrificed her health to this unsupportive relationship. She was not in touch with what she wanted in her life.

We often don't realize that what is going on in our home is a reflection of what is going on inside of us. The home is a mirror to our soul. If we take the time to reflect in our inner space, we can get clear in our outer space.

Clara had lost touch with her personal boundaries in her relationship with her partner, and this was reflected in her home. Her weak Earth Element needed support. I suggested she "get grounded"—that she walk barefoot at the beach and collect some stones and place them next to her bed. I gave her a meditation to help her clarify what she desired in life. And to increase her health and vitality, her yang chi, I suggested that she move her home office desk to a place in the sun.

My longer-term practical recommendation was that she move into the other house as soon as possible. It took eighteen months, but she finally did move out and ended that relationship. She was able to draw her personal boundaries and staked a claim to her health and happiness.

Janet and the Metaphor of Boundaries

Janet had a thriving psychotherapy practice and a large, close extended family, with lots of nieces and nephews. She was everyone's favorite aunt. She contacted me for a feng shui consultation to sate her curiosity about the subject and as a way to move past some issues in her life.

She was looking to develop a support structure. Janet said that although she has some friends, they were not reliable. In addition, her adult nieces and nephews accepted the generosity of her money and time, yet were never able to help her when she reached out to them.

Janet's True Nature was Earth, which gave her the compassion and kindness she needed for her patients. She was a wonderfully nurturing person and provided stability for her extended family. But as sometimes happens with Earth types, her Earth was out of balance. She was perhaps too helpful and available, not allowing people in her life to develop their own self-sufficiency. In her words, she often "bailed out" her family when they were in trouble, and in that process, they never fully learned how to effectively care for themselves. On her part, she often felt bitter and even used when there was little or no expression of gratitude.

She was so intent on keeping the peace in her family, she found she was always extending herself, even with great hardship. She seemed to bend over backward whenever the request was made. And she realized that her family had come to take advantage of her. She didn't know what to do. In other words, Janet's personal boundaries were very weak. She hadn't developed her ability to say no. In fact, just the thought of saying no made her feel selfish and guilty.

In connection with the Earth imbalance, her Fire was out of balance as well. She cared more for others than she did herself. She was not nurturing to herself, and in her own words, "I don't really love who I am." She confessed that helping others was her way of getting love, when really it often made her feel worse.

An Earth imbalance can present in the home environment as lacking physical boundaries on the property or inside the home.

When I toured her property, we discussed the fact that there was no physical separation between her yard and her neighbors'. Only a few shrubs filled in for that role. She said that she did feel a bit exposed (her words) in the back and loved the idea of installing a proper fence.

I had also asked Janet to furnish a sketch of the floor plan of her home. The process can sometimes illuminate how clients really feel about their homes. In this case it provided an interesting clue for Janet's consultation. She drew in doors for all of the upstairs bedrooms with the exception of hers. In fact, she doubled the width of the hallway outside of her bedroom, in effect making her bedroom look as if it was a great open space with no privacy. However, as we walked through the home, I noticed that this was not how things really looked: she had a standard-size hallway and a door. This really pointed out the impact of the Earth imbalance in her life: she felt no separation between herself and others. Her lack of boundaries was making her "too available."

I noticed that neither Janet's bed nor desk was in the ideal position for prospect and refuge or the command position we discussed earlier in this chapter. Her headboard was along the door wall, which did not give her the ability to see the open doorway from bed. On a subconscious level, this position makes us feel vulnerable and unable to completely rest. It can eventually lead to insomnia and sometimes illness.

The same was true for her desk in the home office. Janet, as people often do, uses a spare guest room as her home office, and in doing so, she wanted to maximize the space by placing the desk up against the wall. In this position, her back was to the door and she would not see anyone coming up behind her. Again, this is an unempowered position and impacts her ability to be at her best.

Janet's home was lovely and inviting, as well as very neat and tidy. But I have come to know another Earth imbalance tendency is to cram spaces with stuff—even hidden clutter. Also, Earth is related to kitchens (nurturing) and the center of the home. So as we walked around, with her permission I opened cabinet and closet doors and observed.

I noticed that Janet's refrigerator was full almost to overflowing, even though she was the only person that lived there. A closet under the stairs in the center of her home was so overloaded with clutter that things literally fell out when I opened the door.

As part of my recommendations, I suggested that Janet install the fence in her yard. I suggested that she create a sanctuary in the yard with a garden in a space that particularly drew her attention. I recommended that she create a pebble path to a special, cozy seating area and spend some quality time there.

I asked her to reposition both her bed and desk, so that she could be in full command position. I suggested that she clear out the refrigerator and the closet under the stairs and perhaps get some storage solutions to keep what she really needed in a more orderly manner.

She loved these recommendations and made all the fixes to help her rebalance the Earth in her life. In her meditation practice she worked with the Fire Meditation on page 106 to deepen her Fire and open herself up to self-acceptance and love. She wore a smoky quartz crystal to keep her grounded during the day as a reminder of balanced, stable Earth, and she painted her bedroom a beautiful brownish coral, supporting both Fire and Earth.

Janet acknowledged her underlying issues and had a greater presence of mind in interactions with her family. She did regain that sense of empowerment, strength, and self-love that is such a challenge for many of us! Janet's relationship with her family shifted in a positive way, and they were able to communicate with greater respect and awareness. And she has realized the power of saying a gentle no.

GROUND YOUR EARTH POWER!

Unfortunately, Earth imbalance has been very common among my female clients. It doesn't matter if they are mothers or sisters, aunts or friends; they are often way too giving of their time and energy, compromising their ability to feel good about themselves. Their self-esteem is wrapped up in helping others and being needed. Too much Earth in our personalities will create stagnation and an inability to change. We will experience a life lacking opportunities and vibrancy.

On the other hand, too little Earth manifests as someone who is selfish or untrustworthy. She may be unreliable and irresponsible or lacking in care for the well-being of others. She may be too self-absorbed to see that others around her may need support.

If your Earth is out of balance, ground yourself with the suggestions in this chapter. Bring the Earth Element into your home with some stonework. Collect some beautiful rocks or crystals and place them by your desk or your bed.

If you have too much Earth, the most important thing I can suggest is that you stop and contemplate your relationships. Perhaps you need to find some balance, while pulling back a bit. Are your relationships honoring you? Do you feel whole? Are you reaching out and accepting help from others?

In fashion, Earth is represented by yellow, beige, brown, and peach, and comfortable and classic clothing such as a tweed blazer and khaki pants. Think fabrics with plaid patterns or horizontal lines, as well as jewelry with stones and crystals.

If you don't have enough Earth, consider where you may not be supportive of others. How can you demonstrate your care to others in a loving way? Perhaps you can offer to help someone going through a major challenge in their life. Consider volunteering your time to an organization. Often when we help others, we can put our own challenges in perspective.

Earth in balance is a beauty to behold! She is empathetic, reliable, and stable. She is the one that everyone runs to when they are upset. She has a huge, loving shoulder to cry on. We all need powerful "Earth Mamas," be they men or women. She strives to make her environment harmonious and wants everyone to feel at ease, peaceful, and heard.

Chapter 8

The Metal Element

If you are irritated by every rub, how will you be polished?
—Rumi

Let's review what we've learned about Metal. Metal represents the purity of the precious minerals found deep within the earth after millions of years of compression, heat, and pressure. Through erosion, these minerals flow into our water and nourish it, providing us with vital nutrients.

Metal represents form and function, beauty and order. It helps us create the structures of society as well as beauty in our lives. We can incorporate Metal into our homes with the natural metals found in the Earth as well as man-made metals, including brass, iron, and copper. The energy of Metal represents the spiritual path from awareness to enlightenment. The ultimate and most coveted of these options is gold, a metal that has been equated with divine enlightenment. In Buddhism, the ultimate mineral is diamond. The Diamond Sutra is recited and studied in Mahayana and Zen Buddhism for quickening enlightenment. It is the diamond that "cuts through the illusions" of this material world.

The Metal Element is associated with the heavens, the air, and the sky. Metal is stardust. It is refined and noble. It is the cool, crisp, clean air of late autumn. The sweet aroma of decaying leaves on the forest floor represents the process of contracting and withdrawing in nature. Metal is associated with early evening as coolness takes over.

Metal is related to the lungs, our breath, and the alchemical process of converting various elements into nourishment for our bodies.

Pay attention to the words used to describe Metal personalities in this chapter. Is it your True Nature Element?

SHINY AND CLEAR

Metal is associated with fluctuations of the wind and movement in the sky. It's the circulation of fresh air in our homes allowed by open windows.

Metal is related to the significance of beauty and order in our lives. We seek out that which is beautiful in nature—those spaces that evoke wonder and awe. We are transfixed by the glory of a sunset and admire a well-developed garden. Beauty is essential for an abundant life and achieving our highest abilities.

Metal is reflected in the use of patterns with complexity and order such as fractals. Fractals, also known as sacred geometry, are mathematical shapes and geometric patterns that modern science now identifies as the building blocks of the universe. Although similar in type, they vary widely in scale. Found throughout all of nature's beings, they are something that we recognize as comfortable and familiar to us. They create symmetry and a natural flow.

You can see these patterns in natural materials such as the grain of wood or the spiral of a nautilus shell. There are some very cool home decor items that evoke fractal patterns, such as lighting shaped like branches of coral, leaf patterns in crown molding, paintings of mandalas, and other decorative objects.

THE METAL ARCHETYPE: THE ALCHEMIST

Practiced throughout Europe, Africa, and Asia primarily in the Middle Ages, alchemy's goal was to magically transform ordinary "base" metals into gold, the "noble" metal. The aim was to purify and perfect, which eventually extended to the purification of our souls and the search for an elixir of immortality. Alchemy was the precursor of the modern sciences of chemistry and medicine, while the more philosophical aspects evolved into psychology and esoteric studies. Alchemy was and still is a common metaphor for spiritual enlightenment.

Metal Is Authority and Leadership

Although Metal types are both male and female, Metal is the archetype of the Father energy. He provides strength, yet adaptability—when in balance, Metal knows when to let things flow rather than grasping for the reins. His leadership skills sprout from his confidence and ability to organize others around a project. Always seeking what is right, he has great judgment. He takes what is given and transforms it to the highest level.

This Metal reminds me of a client I had when I was a freelance marketing specialist. She had a commanding presence, not unlike a father-type energy. She was a natural leader and thrived on setting strategy and tactics for new projects. I guess it was my Metal Element that really connected with her, and I loved to be a part of her wonderfully organized work. Having been in this career for a couple of decades, I truly appreciated the skills and talent that she brought to her projects.

. . . Or Domineering

Metal can be domineering, like the archetype of the Father, rigidly holding to his position. He sees only black or white—he does not allow for the subtle nuances of gray. He can be too formal and distant among peers, and his communication may be too blunt and direct.

On the other hand, he may be unable to speak up against injustice, allowing others to walk all over him or others that he holds dear.

Metal Is the Moral Compass

He gives us virtue and discretion and holds others to their highest standard. He will fight dearly for what he believes is fairness and equality for all. Metal gives us virtue and discretion.

I am reminded of an experience I had when I was around thirteen. I was walking with a group of friends, when one of them threw a candy wrapper on the street. I was disgusted and reacted sharply, telling her that she shouldn't do that. Immediately I regretted it, thinking that I might be ostracized from the group (oh, the pitfalls of self-esteem at thirteen!). However, to my surprise, my friend bent down and picked up the wrapper. And to this day, we are the best of friends, remembering how it was a minor turning point in our young lives. We all need such experiences to see how we need to take a stand for what is right, regardless of the consequences.

. . .Or Can Be Self-Righteous or Hypocritical

Metal may be intolerant of others opinions and staunchly hold to his ideals. He can behave punitively to those that do not uphold them. With his blunt communication style he can drive people away. Or he may be hypocritical and not follow through on his convictions.

At another great turning point in my friend Matt's life, he became aware that his self-righteous behavior was challenging his closest relationships. This excessive Metal was a reaction to feeling powerless. He felt that he alone had the right perspective when he was actually being very narrow-minded. He explains that in his failed attempts to change others' behavior he became very punishing to them, which only exacerbated the situation. He finally became conscious of his poor behavior through a dream. It showed him very clearly that other people were also "divine" and their presence in his life was, among other reasons, to teach him an important lesson in self-awareness.

Metal Is Structure
and Organization

Metal possesses a great logical mind. He has a skill in filtering what is no longer needed. Metal provides strength, yet adaptability when in balance, knowing when to let things flow rather than holding them tight. He is precise in his expression and work. He is a rule maker and a rule follower.

One of Matt's greatest strengths is structure and organization. It came in very handy while developing the education materials for his coaching program. Creating a logical path for the topics to be covered, laying out the content for each module, as well as organizing a system for students to translate this material were easy for him.

But it's taken him a while to see that the way he was teaching was still coming from that logical brain, not his intuitive mind. He needed to learn to break from the shackles of the content and all the details (Metal) and engage every one of his students with the psychological teachings and often life-changing perspectives that one collides with in a program of this nature. He needed to channel the energy of Water (to go more with the flow and a feeling/ emotional path) and Fire (to engage his students and light *their* fire) when he taught.

. . . Or Can Be a Perfectionist

Metal can be too strict and not a go-with-the-flow type. He can be a perfectionist to the extreme and unable to settle for anything less. He may have obsessive compulsive disorder. He can be oversensitive to his environment—sounds, scents, visuals, tactile sensations, as well as vibrational energy—and either detach or soak up the bad vibes. He may not be able to release sadness and grief, which will be held in his lungs. He may develop asthma and other breathing difficulties in response to the stored-up grief.

Metal Is Beauty and Refinement

Metal admires beauty and refinement. He tends to be very sensitive to his environment through all of his senses. He often surrounds himself with fine art and music. Metal is a connoisseur of the finest things in life. He filters and refines, easily removing all that is no longer needed.

I see the Metal Element in my brother-in-law Dave when it comes to wine. He has created—I'm sure without realizing the profound significance of it—a beautiful ritual and ceremony surrounding the wine experience. All of the senses are stimulated. The wineglasses are cleaned and dried in a ritualistic way. Care is taken that each glass is of the highest purity. Then comes the selection of the bottle and discussion about its variety, vineyard, and vintage. The opening of the bottle is a dramatic moment. In fact, cork has the best effect—one Metal wine friend says that the sound of popping the cork stimulates the relaxation response in her! Pouring a glass and observing the bouquet provoke the senses of sight and smell. All of this is for the anticipation of having the first sip. It's a beauty to behold!

The Japanese tea ceremony is another beautiful demonstration of the grace and power of the Metal Element. I participated in an abbreviated ceremony at a local college. Every movement, every instrument, every connection was handled with great mindfulness, precision, honor, and respect. And that respect extended to everything, including the handmade tools.

Metal Is Simplicity

Metal desires simplicity and minimalism. An aesthetic monk is the poster child of Metal. He dismisses material excesses, living in an austere space with bare essentials. Metal can also be a modern design devotee with the sleek, ultra modern decor found in many interior design magazines.

. . . Or Can Be Too Austere

However, Metal's purity and strict adherence to form over function can sometimes be punishing, lacking in comfort and balance. Visitors may feel unwelcome and unable to relax.

Metal Is Connection to the Sacred

The true Alchemist, Metal strives for purity and divine connection. He is on a spiritual path and helps others align with their spirituality. Connected to the angelic realm, his passion for ceremony and refinement creates an air of sacredness.

Metal is attracted to careers requiring precision, such as accounting, architecture, and medicine. They are also great in careers involved in beauty such as interior design and fashion. With their ability to lead and organize, they are often C-level executives in organizations.

Metal often has some of these facial attributes: a well-defined nose, prominent upper cheeks, visible upper lids, wider space between facial features, moles, and a pale complexion. He tends to have fine bones and holds himself regally.

In Metal's home, there is cleanliness and organization. The home feels light and airy and walls are often white with splashes of artwork.

Strengths and Weaknesses

Strengths—Leadership, planning, organizing, creating structure from nothing, methodical, discerning, calm, disciplined, great with follow-through, precise, detail-oriented, respects authority, reasonable, logical, holds self and others to the highest standard.

Weaknesses—Self-critical, perfectionist, self-righteous, austere, petty, needs guidelines and rules, complains to a fault/unable to break rules, needs control, everything is black and white, dislikes change, unable to see the big picture.

Physical symptoms of weak Metal are frailty, shortness of breath, congestion, delicate skin, and loss of body hair. Too much Metal manifests as dry skin and hair, a stiff spine and neck, cracked lips, and sinus headaches.

Metal is created by the condensing and hardening of soil, the Earth Element. It is controlled or melted by Fire. For instance, the exuberance of Fire blasts through the carefully laid-out strategy and discipline of the Metal Element. Metal's life-giving nutrients create nourishing Water from which all life springs. The discernment and sharpness of Metal keeps the impulsivity of Wood in check, therefore Metal controls Wood.

In our lives, the Metal Element represents the completion of creative projects and harvesting of the fruits of our labor, including our work, the arts, and children. It signifies support and helpful people, including friends, mentors, clients, coworkers, and neighbors. Metal also represents purity and connection with the divine. It symbolizes the spiritual alchemical process of transformation and higher consciousness and provides us with divine wisdom and guidance.

THE METAL ELEMENT IN THE HOME

The Metal Element plays a vital role in our homes to model cleanliness, precision, morality and order in our lives.

Objects and furnishings made from metal material are a powerful representation of this Element. Just like overdone Fire can create imbalance in a home, be careful not to accumulate too much Metal. One piece of furniture or a few silver objects on your mantel are great. Too much Metal can feel stark and austere (picture an all-white ultramodern room in a magazine).

Metal is represented by colors ranging from white and gray to silver and gold. Metal colors are great as a good neutral backdrop on walls that will showcase other objects in the room. Too much Metal will feel cold. So be sure to add touches of color with fabrics or artwork.

Circles, ovals, and arches are another way to bring the Metal Element into our homes. The circle represents heaven and brings softness to our environments. I often suggest purchasing round or oval tables to offset an abundance of straight lines—balancing the yin and yang.

Metal artwork can take the form of a metal sculpture, images of the sky, or masculine or angelic images. The art objects are often very carefully presented in a gallery setting or groupings.

Metal Is Structure and Organization

Keeping your home tidy and clean is a clear indication of the Metal Element in action. The Metal person is fastidious and everything has its place. He has all the storage solutions appropriate for his things and household items. He labels everything so that everyone knows where it belongs! The last minutes every night and the first in the morning are spent putting things back where they belong. Clutter is the antithesis of Metal; in fact, it is an indication of a Metal deficiency. Metal in excess obsessively cleans, imagining dirt and germs everywhere.

The Metal Element has a clear presence in homes that feel good. Daily chores—clearing the sink, washing clothes, the polished silver tea set, the floors vacuumed and mopped, the windows cleaned to a sparkling finish—and seasonal maintenance give rise to a well-loved home.

Metal Is Beauty and Refinement

Because Metal people appreciate the finer things in life, their homes often include collections of furnishings, artwork, and/or objects that are of the finest workmanship and quality. Whether they turn out to be a vintage movie poster aficionado or a Jackson Pollock collector, their desire is to have the best of the genre.

Refinement may also show up with appreciation of fine food, wine, music, and dance. A place to enjoy or store their collections such as a wine cellar, music room, or an art studio may also be incorporated in the home.

Metal in Excess can mean homes that are like a museum or a show house—again, it cannot feel welcoming to sit on that antique sofa with über-expensive silk fabric or be afraid you'll knock over a Ming vase. On the other hand, depleted Metal might lead to a home where everything looks cheap and ugly and no attention has been brought to the aesthetics.

Metal Is Simplicity

Often the design choices of strong Metal personalities are simple, modern, and can be very minimalistic. Their homes can provide a simple, stripped-down refuge from a cluttered world. Paring things down to the basics and filtering out the unnecessary—that is what Metal does best. With neutral tones on the walls, the home provides a crisp, clean base that inspires a sense of calm. Sometimes their homes can be so austere as to be unwelcoming. They do not feel lived-in. Metal minimalism can be so extreme as to dispose of anything providing a connection to the past.

I have a good friend whose mother was extreme Metal. She kept a very spartan home. She often threw out my friend's personal belongings. Her house was extremely austere and uncomfortable. There was no artwork from her childhood, no old toys to reminisce about. As a result, my friend compensates for a childhood home that was unwelcoming by being the complete opposite. She is a pack rat, clinging to objects that have outlived their use. She has a story for everything and why she "needs" it.

Metal Is Connection to the Sacred

Metal is connection with the sacred in our everyday lives. Make a space for meditation and prayer. Perhaps create an altar in your home to be a constant reminder of the divine in your daily life.

I placed a small altar in the center of my home as its heart. We walk past it all day long, and it's a gentle reminder of the spirit of place. I put money that I receive for my services, as well as any other checks, photos, thank-you cards, invitations, and even printed emails that are especially important to my career on this altar. My husband and children also place objects on this altar, and we light a candle and give thanks. It is a daily reminder of the sacred in our lives.

THE METAL ELEMENT IN THE GARDEN

A great way to bring the qualities of Metal into our gardens is through hardscape structure and ornamental pieces: a metal gate as an attractive entry to your yard, a metal trellis with rose vines creeping upward, a rusted metal latticework that contrasts with the siding of your home in a porch area, a gazing ball, or a handmade sculpture to provide the yang to the yin of the garden beds.

A set of metal wind chimes and even wrought-iron seating with comfortable cushions will provide touches of Metal to your outdoor space. White flowers (also a symbol for the Metal Element) in your garden bed provide a soft touch. Be mindful of not adding too much of the Metal Element. A little goes a long way. Too much Metal will make the outdoor space feel too cold and harsh.

THE METAL ELEMENT IN NATURE

Being actively aware of the weather patterns creates a connection to the Metal Element. Just noticing the temperature of the air, the changing cloud patterns, and the coolness of the breeze is a great start. But consider our ancestors and all that has nearly been lost to the majority of human beings. They were able to read the sky for subtle changes in movement and watched the constellations as they reflected the shift from one season to another. They paid attention to the subtle smell and quality of the air before a rainstorm or the color of the sky just before a snowfall.

One evening while at a Cub Scout event at the beach, a powerful storm came and tore through our camp. It upended tables and tossed chairs. It collapsed nearly every tent set up for the night. We could see the black clouds approaching for a good half-hour. I was mesmerized and couldn't take my eyes off of the sky. As the wind and rain hit us, it was, I would imagine, as close to a tornado as I've ever come in contact with. It was chaos as we all ran in every direction. In a matter of seconds I did not know where my husband and son had gone. I grabbed my daughter and rushed to the car, yelling over the roar of the wind. It was over in a few minutes, but those few minutes left indelible marks on my psyche. The power of that storm filled me with tremendous awe and sense of the mystery of the natural world. We develop a great respect for that which we cannot control. It was in every way an awesome experience, connecting me with the Divine source.

But you don't have to go through such a dramatic event to connect with the power of the Metal Element in nature.

You can lie out on a blanket and observe the night sky. This is particularly fun if there is a comet event. Or you can observe the sky during the day and watch the clouds pass along. It was fun for all of us in childhood, yet many of us never consider "wasting" time like that as adults.

You can stand on a bluff or mountaintop and feel the power of the wind go through your body's energy field.

You can observe the gleam of the colors of gold and silver from mica in rocks and sand.

In late autumn, take a walk in the woods and breathe in the cool crispness of the air and the sweet scent of decomposing leaves.

SPACE CLEARING AND BLESSING RITUAL

As Metal is our connection to the Divine, it represents the quality of energy of the land. Observe the quality of chi on your property. Does it feel clear and fresh or dull and clouded? If land has positive chi, it will attract an abundance of life, health, relationships, and prosperity. If the chi of the land is depleted, it will create stagnation, illness, and a lack of opportunity in all areas of life.

It is easy to observe the energy of the land. Just sit quietly and open your senses. What feelings do you get? If you sense some disquiet or chaotic stirrings, you probably need to revitalize the land.

There are a variety of space clearing rituals from many indigenous traditions you can do to bring greater chi back to your property. Sometimes just observing that there is negative chi and the intention to heal it are all that is necessary. A space clearing ceremony should include a blessing on the land. When neutralizing negative chi, a vacuum or blank slate that can attract any forces that are around is created. A blessing ceremony fills this empty space with positive intentions and prayer; it is reprogrammed to fulfill a new purpose. These ceremonies are especially important when you move into a home to remove the energy from past occupants and any trauma and infuse the space with intention for you and your family.

To bless the land, simply invoke or call in a connection to all of the natural elements, to the nature spirits, and to Divine Presence. Say a prayer in your heart and visualize white light to fill every space with your positive goals and intentions. For instance, very simplistically, I ask for an abundance of health, prosperity, love, and joy for me and my family and all who enter our land.

Connecting to the heart of your home can start an ongoing dialogue about how you can honor it and how your home will provide for you. Doing regular ceremonies and opening yourself to communication will raise your consciousness and enrich your life.

The Breath

The Metal Element controls the lungs, our breath, and the ability to accept the breath down into the body and release sadness and grief. Metal assists us with modulating and observing the breath when we are in various emotional states. We tend to breathe in a shallow way, which puts us in the fight-or-flight mode. However, when we become aware of the breath, we have the power to transform our emotional states through the parasympathetic system, known as the relaxation response.

In times of anger you can choose to breathe smoothly and freely to remain calm. When anxious or afraid, the breath is restrained. You can consciously broaden and deepen your whole breathing to feel safe. When depressed, fully inhale to match your exhalation to stimulate your chi and help you access the emotions hidden within the depressed behavior. When feeling hurt, under attack, or when old emotional patterns are threatening to take control, get back into the *now* by centering the breath.

ALTERNATE NOSTRIL BREATHING MEDITATION

You can do this technique wherever you are and whenever you want to be calmer. If you do yoga, you may be familiar with this technique in your practice.

With your right hand, rest your pointer and middle finger on your third eye (the space between your eyebrows). Use your thumb to close your right nostril and breathe in through your left. Then close your left nostril with your ring finger and exhale through your right. Then, alternate breathing back and forth, just like this, several times. Along with creating greater calm, this breathing is known to boost mental functioning, soothe the nervous system, and enhance sleep.

CONNECTING HEAVEN AND EARTH MEDITATION

Find a quiet spot and center yourself. Feel the air around you and recognize that the air close to your body is your energy field. Imagine with each inhale that your energy field is expanding until it finally encompasses the room you are in. Continue to expand your energy field until you visualize that the upper portion of it opens to the heavens above. Continue your visualization and feel that the lower portion of your energy field opens to the earth below. Allow the energy of both Heaven (the Creator, the Father) and Earth (the Receptive, the Mother), representing the balance of yin and yang, to merge within you and nourish you.

—From the teachings of H. H. Grandmaster Professor Lin Yun

CASE STUDIES

Busy Beth

Of all of the Five Elements, the most common imbalance to find among women is Earth. Because our culture pushes an ideal mother archetype on us, our self-image can often be one that is severely imbalanced. The traditional role as caregiver can swallow us up if we are not careful. And Earth imbalance is often coupled with a deficiency in Metal, the archetypal Father energy.

Such was the case with Beth. Beth was in her late thirties when I first met her. She had been a dedicated wife and mother, never pursuing a career of outside of her home. She kept herself busy taking care of her large, beautifully designed home and being the typical "soccer mom" shuttling kids from here to there every day. She was primarily interested in making the energy in her home optimal for her husband, as he was an attorney and brought in the only income in the family.

About five years later, I received a phone call from her. She wanted me to help her with a new stage of her life. She was newly separated from her husband and felt lost. She told me about her husband's betrayal and how she felt that she had lost her identity.

She asked me to help her remove the negative energy from the recent breakup and create a positive place for her sons and her to move forward in.

At this consultation, I learned more about Beth. She told me that she had married young and moved away from her childhood home directly into a home with her new husband. She had never made any major decisions on her own and had never managed their finances. She hadn't had the opportunity to fully develop her Metal, which helps with confidence, power, and discernment in decision making.

I recalled that years earlier, while sitting in her kitchen, I had asked Beth where she and her family ate dinner. She told me that they ate around the kitchen counter, because they were always on the go. The stool closest to the kitchen appliances would be Beth's preference so that she could have easy access to the food, but her husband always seemed to take this chair. So instead of moving around the counter to another seat, she always stood while they ate their meals. She said, "I don't mind!" when I told her that standing while she ate dinner was not right. And unfortunately I do hear this type of thing from many female clients.

Her situation demonstrated both Earth and Metal imbalance: self-sacrifice (Earth) and lack of confidence while swallowing injustice, however inconsequential it seemed to her at the time (Metal). One simple action can speak volumes.

This one scenario painted a larger picture of their relationship, which was an omen about the breakup of their marriage. Now Beth was fearing change (Earth) and loss of control while unable to express her grief and feeling vulnerable (Metal).

At the consultation, I was happy to hear that Beth had recently enrolled in an energy healing program with a friend. She had decided to do it at the insistence of her friend but hadn't realized the full extent of the program. As with any esoteric training, this program requires participants to delve into their own inner psyche, some for the first time in their lives!

The combination of mind-body-spirit work, meditation and stillness, and journaling exercises was beyond what Beth thought she could handle. Deep down her spirit craved the connection with the sacred (Metal), but she acknowledged that she was approaching the class with a reserved detachment (also Metal). The program stirred anxiety in her. Perhaps it was too much, too soon for her.

Some people would rather visit the dentist than take some time to be alone with their thoughts. Because I have a strong Water Element in my personality—which loves contemplation—this reaction is foreign to me, but I know that some find going within to be a scary place. Many have spent their lives "other-focused" and believing that being "self-focused" is indulgent and selfish.

Unbalanced Earth contributes to weak Metal. Beth was stuck, yet change was forced upon her from the outside. She strove for self-awareness, yet recoiled when it got too ugly. She seemed overwhelmed by the lack of control in her life.

To get a feeling of control back, Beth talked about doing some new renovations to the house. Her renovations seemed unnecessary, perhaps a way to keep herself busy with small decisions. However, it might also build her decision making skills and strengthen her Metal.

As part of Beth's training program, she was to meditate and recite mantras on a daily basis. I suggested that she create a space in her bedroom for this inner work, so she could have privacy and make the room feel like a sanctuary so she could allow the feelings of vulnerability that would inevitably arise.

I reviewed each of the boys' bedrooms and suggested moving their beds into command position to provide them with a feeling of empowerment (we discussed this in the Earth Element chapter). I also suggested some color changes in their rooms to support their True Nature Elements. This would help her boys adapt to this major change in their lives.

I recommended that she consider making room for herself in the house outside of her bedroom. Having been surrounded by all-male energy for twenty-plus years, she never considered creating a space for herself. I suggested that she turn her husband's home office into a place for her yoga and meditation practice—somewhere she could close the door and feel safe and nourished. I recommended she paint the room a cream color to help lighten up the dark space and regain balance with her Earth Element. Placement of a mirror there would also amplify the natural light and reflect the beautiful gardens she had in her yard. I also suggested reinforcing the Earth Element with a bowl of rocks or a few quartz crystals and artwork displaying a powerful mountain that she loved to feel like she finally owned the space with inner strength.

I gave her the Alternate Nostril Breathing Meditation (p. 152) to help her calm anxiety and to allow the lungs to open up and process her grief. In addition, I suggested that she notice and observe the sky and its changing color and shapes at night and during the day. Connecting with the heavens would help her to reconnect with her Metal spirit and feel her power!

Cathy Gets the Connections

Cathy called me to do a consultation to help her attract a long-term romantic partner and to enhance her business. In the past decade, Cathy had had several relationships, and all of them eventually moved out and moved on.

She was an interior designer and known for her talent in creating beautiful spaces. Although she had attracted a good clientele, she had also gotten a reputation as being difficult to work with and her business suffered. It was her uncompromising ethic and need for perfection that both contributed to her success and subsequent challenges. Cathy held tightly to her business policies, and her highly critical nature turned some clients and their future referrals away.

Cathy's True Nature was Metal, and it was her overdeveloped, heavy Metal that was overwhelming her other Elements.

Cathy is a beautiful woman with classic, sophisticated styling. She was very refined and "put together," yet understated. In our discussion about her relationships both personal and business, I immediately saw in her the archetype of the domineering father figure. She treated everyone as if they were children who absolutely needed her guidance and direction. She alone had the answers and was not open to hearing other perspectives.

As I toured her home, I was struck by the decor. The house was so clean and neat that you could literally eat off the gleaming bleached-wood floors. Her home looked like it was right out of a design magazine spread—all white, chrome, and polish. She had added some subtle light colors, such as baby blue and sage green, in a few throw pillows and a few pieces of art. Even her bedroom was all white—white walls, white linens, and a few black-and-white photographs.

The entire home was very yang: all Metal and completely out of balance with the other four Elements. And, as usual, her home was a perfect metaphor for her life. She had created a life that was very controlled, even "cold" and orderly, not allowing space for the flexibility of Wood, the passion of Fire, the nurturing of Earth, or the self-contemplation of Water.

After we spent some time together, we talked about the concept of her home being a mirror of her life. She started to see the connection with the strength of Metal, which she quickly identified with and loved about herself. I explained the Five Elements and their relationships to each other and the need for greater balance between them. And the big win in our discussion was that she saw the logic (Metal) in requiring that balance not only in her home environment, but also in her personal inner environment.

Since Metal can have a strong desire for divine connection, I suggested a breathing exercise. Metal's energy is about the contraction and conservation of energy, just as a tree's energy pulls back and inward in late fall preparing for winter. Overstimulated Metal is about holding in the breath and the emotion of grief. I gave her the Connecting to Heaven and Earth Meditation (p. 153), which focuses on the opposing energies of expansion and merging. It facilitates the opening up of our energy fields to connect both yin and yang. It would help her bring her contracted, intense Metal back into balance. I suggested that she create an altar to do this daily meditation practice at.

It was clear that Cathy was not going to radically change the design of her home, so I suggested some subtle additions of the other Elements in her space: Live plants for the Wood Element can magically change the feel of a stark white environment. I suggested a water fountain in her foyer to open up the flow of opportunities into her home. Wood is the grandchild of Metal and so can soften its energy, along with Water, which softly drains Metal.

She placed a few touches of Fire in her bedroom to help with romance, such as a few throw pillows on her bed and two candles on the nightstand. She also added a few crystals to bring in the Element of Earth. In her home office we added Fire to generate energy by changing out the frames of her prints to ones with a leopard pattern, and Earth and Wood with stone vases to hold fresh flowers.

Not long after our consultation, Cathy met a wonderful man and still shares her life with him. Her business is doing better now, and she gets lots of referrals. She told me how learning about feng shui really opened her up to understanding energy, especially the energy of relationships.

POLISH YOUR METAL POWER!

Too much Metal is like a tree in late autumn—contracted, decaying energy that lacks vitality. The focus is on what's right, in order, and perfect, without care for the human beings involved or their ideas and contributions. Heavy Metal is the punitive, strict parent who lashes out at our every inadequacy. On the other hand, weak Metal lacks authority and, in fact, looks to others for authority and structure. Weak Metal does not want to make any decisions, lacks confidence, and fears failure. He does not speak up when witnessing injustice. He blends into the crowd for fear of being singled out.

Balanced Metal keeps our societies morally right and structurally sound. It provides leadership and efficiency, while maintaining beauty and clarity in the environment. Balanced Metal reminds us of clear expression, poise, and refinement.

If you want to reclaim your Metal power, you can wear clothing that represents Metal, such as sharp, sophisticated designer clothes. If you don't have the high-end budget, Metal can make a low-budget outfit look divine! Whatever the price tag, Metal Element clothes are tailored and hang well on the body. Metal fabrics include those with sheen and sparkle, such as silk, as well as the colors of white, gray, gold, and silver. Accessories include chunky metal jewelry and round pendants.

You can start with decluttering your home. If necessary, bring in a professional. Once you have organized what is left, perform a space clearing and blessing ritual to refresh and enhance the energy of your home. Place an altar in a conspicuous spot so that you have a daily connection to the sacred. Observe the sky, night and day. Notice the changes as the day moves through the hours. Notice the seasonal changes of the constellations. Be aware of the fall when vegetation follows the Metal energy of contraction and decay. Notice the wildlife responding to the shifts in weather patterns, such as the leaves turning colors and falling into bountiful piles and the geese flying south for winter. Make breath work or meditation part of your daily practice to go within and to release what is no longer necessary in your life. Be shiny and clear!

Chapter 9

The Water Element

*A lake is the landscape's most beautiful and expressive feature.
It is earth's eye; looking into which the beholder measures the
depth of his own nature.*

—Henry David Thoreau

Let's review what we have learned about the Water Element so far. Of all the Elements, Water is the most precious. We cannot survive more than a few days without it. It quenches thirst and allows for reflection. It can be deep and still like a lake, or wild and flowing like a waterfall. Water matches the rhythm of our bodies to the rhythm of the tides of the ocean. Blood flowing through our veins is like the water flowing through the veins of the earth. Where there is water, there is life.

We were created in Water, and our bodies are 70 percent water. So is the Earth. Water is conductive and absorbs and disperses energy.

We gravitate to Water, as it refreshes and renews us. Our most holy rituals in the world's religions include renewal in water. We are programmed to identify healthy land with abundant and clear water.

Water makes up half of feng shui's meaning: *wind and water.* It is synonymous with wealth, prosperity, and abundance. There is a close relationship between mountains and water in feng shui.

Mountains are symbolic of the bones in the body. Water is symbolic of blood flowing inside the body, distributing nourishment. Similarly, water carries earthly chi to the land. Water is the bringer of chi, and mountains are the container.

Water is formless yet powerful. It can be the roar of a tidal wave or fall gently as rain. It can be the expanse of the ocean or a puddle in the street. Water is mysterious and dangerous. It gives life, yet is destructive. We will not soon forget the destructive power of the water in Hurricane Katrina and the tsunamis of Sri Lanka and Japan. Water gives, and water takes away.

But physical water is only part of this chi. The energy of Water and what it represents in nature are of greater significance. The movement of Water is varied: descending as rain, flowing, spilling over, still, frozen, lapping on a shore, seeking the lowest level, filling up, absorbing energy, taking on the shape of a container, reflective and internal. Water is the most yin of all of the Five Elements. It is associated with winter and midnight—cold, dark, and still. Water represents death and rebirth. It is the womb and the promise of a new life. Water is the feminine, the dream world, the moon.

Do Water personality traits resonate with you? Pay attention to the wording used in this chapter for the True Nature Assessment coming up in part three.

WABI SABI AND FLOW

Water is related to good flow and the natural authenticity of our spaces, as well as mystery and peril.

Like a river, chi flows. Chi flows like water, down the roads, through your neighborhood, down your street, and up the pathway to your front door. Is there no direct path to your front door? You are definitely losing opportunities for chi to enter your life. The path is the water and the doorway is the access point. Be sure that you have a pathway to your front door. Better yet, have a softly, curving path made of natural material such as peat or stone.

Chi enters through all the doors and windows of our homes, but the front door is the primary portal, providing nourishment for all spaces. Make sure that there are no obstacles to allow the smooth flow of chi.

Imagine the chi flowing through the hallways through your home. Just like a river, feel yourself to be the energy that moves throughout the pathways. It is important to be aware of any blockages in the hallways. I do not recommend placing furnishings in hallways, unless the items are very shallow in depth and/or the hallway is wider than the standard thirty-six inches. Is there anything that clogs up the pathway, requiring you to walk around it? Is there a table that you constantly bump your hip or shin on when you walk by?

Having an easy flow throughout your home is good for yin. For efficiency, most homes and furniture are built with straight lines, so introducing curves wherever you can helps to restore balance and comfort. A round table, a curved buffet, or rounded corners on your granite kitchen counter create a smoother flow of chi.

Research shows that we are calmed by curves and bored when confronted with straight lines. We can also feel threatened with pointed objects. Our homes are built with straight lines and right angles. But worse, some newer homes incorporate slanted walls (walls with obtuse angles of greater than ninety degrees). These spaces are jarring to our senses. Curves mimic nature; nothing in nature has straight lines. Incorporating curves into your decor wherever possible is a good choice.

Water's energy is to go within, to float within those inner spaces and return back to the surface with what's real, authentic, and genuine. It embodies the Japanese aesthetic of Wabi Sabi. It's the rustic simplicity of handmade objects produced with natural materials. It's the celebration of the wear and patina on our objects and furnishings over years of loving use. Often called the "wisdom of natural simplicity," wabi sabi relates to the quirkiness and uniqueness that is inherent in the Water Element.

In the *I-Ching*, or *Book of Changes*, Water is known as "The Abysmal," the dangerous. Water embues a sense of mystery and peril in our lives. We can create that sense of mystery in our home by designing a curved pathway with a partially obstructed view that leads to an unknown destination. A pond or waterfall that evokes "safe" danger in the subconscious mind mimics our experience in the natural world.

THE WATER ARCHETYPE: THE PHILOSOPHER

The Water Element loves stillness and contemplation. In a culture that glorifies the activity and competitiveness of the Wood Element, Water provides inner reflection, an opportunity to replenish our energy, and prioritizes ample time for sleep and dreams. Proper Water gives us a feeling of security and the ability to process fear from the past, present, or future. Balancing the Water Element is crucial in our lives, to help us restore our energy and feel nourished and supported. Water is independent and prefers to work alone on her own time. Water also provides the space for idea generation and planning, where ideas plant their seed (as in the womb), waiting to emerge from the ground when the timing is right.

Water Is Deep and Introverted

An introvert, Water requires and craves time alone for deep reflection and contemplation. Water ponders the mysteries of life and the big existential questions. She is the Philosopher! Always a student, she craves knowledge and seeks the perfect teacher. She easily transitions from one dimension to another—the spiritual plane is but a finger-length away. She flows, seeking the deepest level and lowest places.

Water also knows the importance of sleep to maintain a healthy lifestyle and longevity. It allows the brain to strengthen memory, spurs creativity, sharpens our focus, and gives us a greater ability to reduce stress and decrease moodiness. Sleep also improves metabolism and enhances our immune systems to ward off disease. Water nurtures herself, understanding the need to balance the yang with the yin.

I am a Leo, and I have always related to the Fire Element. But as I learned about the Five Elements, I soon came to realize the significance of Water, the Philosopher, in my life.

Looking back I can see how the Water Element truly influenced my young life and does still to this day. My father died when I was eleven, and fairly soon after I became very contemplative and philosophical. Now, of course, I recognize the significance of my father's death as a treasured gift in my spiritual awakening. I dove into astrology soon after, on a path of understanding myself and my purpose in life. I craved my alone time, yet balanced it with my need to socialize and be on stage (Fire).

. . . Or Can Always Be Searching

Water can be so obsessed with the big questions, she is always searching and never feeling satisfied. She knows that the bottom is fathomless, yet she doesn't hesitate to attempt to reach it. She can be obsessed with death and the afterlife and not able to live in the present moment. She is unable to relate to people who don't share her passions.

Megan has been a friend of mine for about twenty years, since I committed to my spiritual path in earnest. She often finds it hard to relate to people that live on the surface of life and doesn't have any patience for them. It's a real challenge for her as an energy healer because she often has to deal with clients who believe that healing comes from outside themselves. Those people want to pay someone to heal them, but don't want to change their way of thinking or their lifestyle. Fortunately, as she's evolved and grown, she has found herself surrounded by more like-minded people, giving her a wonderful network of those in sync with her passion for depth. And this community provides the deep well to draw from to truly help others.

Water Is Independent and Self-Sufficient

Water actually prefers to work alone in nonconventional careers. A nonconformist, she abhors tradition for tradition's sake. She prefers working in a freelance consulting capacity. Water "beats her own drum." She does things her way regardless of what others think. She rarely shares her opinions with others and, therefore, feels no obligation to listen to the opinions of others.

This, too, rings so true for Megan. After college, she went the traditional route of getting a full-time job in technology. She worked the 9-to-5 routine for a while, but when she had children, she strove to work part-time even after her colleagues said it was impossible in her field. But she persisted and wound up doing just that and making good money for most of her career. Now as a healer, Megan is in her flow as a solo entrepreneur. This is perfect for her Water nature!

. . . Or Can Be Inaccessible and Isolated

Water may spend so much time alone that she is isolated from society, a sort of hermit. She then becomes unable to relate to others and may be lonely. She may be highly critical and skeptical of others' motives and behavior. She is very private and feels vulnerable and so can easily get overwhelmed.

One thing that Megan was concerned about after leaving the corporate world was feeling isolated in her solo entrepreneur gig. She immediately realized that she needed community (Fire) and joined a few organizations and volunteered on their directorial boards. These experiences have prevented her from feeling isolated and lonely.

Water Is Imaginative and Playful

Without bounds, her deep internal access and contemplation gives her great imagination and creativity. Water is often the artist—the painter, musician, poet—even if this isn't her occupation. Typically shy, she has the capacity to inspire others if she is shares her work with them. Her brilliance shines through.

In a nontraditional sense, Water is creative by coming up with alternative solutions to problems. She is like the stream encountering a boulder. She builds up her energy and finds her way around it. When in balance, Water has a great playfulness, like a small babbly brook. She is not afraid of letting her artistry flow without judgment.

Megan says that she always felt that she lacked creativity. Her childhood friend had all the artistic talent. They did many arts and crafts together, and her thingamabobs always looked sad compared to her friend's. Megan was very artistic (Water) but seemed to have the gift of perfectionism (Metal). It took many years for her to *feel* creative, but once she started to view herself this way, she really enjoyed expressing that with watercolors. I believe that we are all creative. We just need to find where our creativity lies, then tap into it and enjoy where it takes us!

. . . Or Can Be Eccentric

Water has great creativity, but without a balance in her life and interaction with others, she can become that eccentric "cat lady." She may feel sorrow and loneliness or ostracized if she doesn't reach out to others.

Water Is Calm and Flowing

A great asset of Water is that she brings a sense of calmness to any situation. Others rely on her ability to see the big picture and not get caught up with the details. Her energy is fluid, and often people say she "goes with the flow."

. . . Or Can Be Suspicious and Cynical

When Water is imbalanced, she retreats in fear from others. She becomes overprotective and suspicious of others' motives and behavior. Unbalanced Water is cynical and feels unsafe in her surroundings. In the extreme, she can become reclusive and develop phobias. At the extremes, she can be always home (too little Water) or never home (too much Water).

The archetype of Water (The Philosopher) is seen in our poets and philosophers from time immemorial. They are the thinkers, sages, and wise teachers as well as the witches and shamans that were ostracized, living on the edges of society. They are the ones that thought outside the box, recognizing that the Earth was not flat and, in fact, that our bodies are made up of microscopic cells.

People who have a Water True Nature tend to be freelancers or consultants. They prefer to make their own schedules. They are often in imaginative-type work, in the arts or esoteric fields, or quantum physics. Unlike Fire, which craves the stage, Water types tend to be in the background, writing screenplays, in the laboratories, or designing websites. They are drawn to teaching positions, giving them the opportunity to constantly go deeper themselves.

Water types often have some of these facial/body features: a prominent chin, high forehead, puffiness and/or shadows around eyes, large ears/lobes. Body type tends to be plump with strong bones, wavy/thick hair, with black undertones to skin (regardless of race).

Physical symptoms of weak Water are dulled vision and hearing, feeling cold, osteoporosis, lacking appetite, headaches. Like Water, she can be dried up or frozen. Too much Water can lead to headaches, lack of perspiration, or rigidity of muscles and joints.

Her home houses lots of books and her own journals. It is filled with original artwork and creative projects abound. Her meditation space is of primary importance, but don't expect her to give you a tour. She keeps her private spaces to herself.

Strengths and Weaknesses

Strengths—Great thinker, curious, imaginative, creative, dreamer, independent, careful, thrifty, sensible, playful, articulate, clever, self-sufficient, analytical, conceives, seeks knowledge and truth, self-knowledge, can go with the flow.

Weaknesses—Difficulty with initiating, blunt, withdrawn, fearful, critical, detached, suspicious, demanding, unforgiving, cynical, preoccupied, eccentric, distrustful, insecure, introverted.

Water is nourished by the Metal Element. Water's tendency to flow in all directions is channeled and contained by Earth. Water nourishes the Wood Element, therefore its chi is drained by Wood. Water douses the Fire Element, therefore it controls Fire.

In our lives, Water represents our chosen career, independence, and our personal journey.

THE WATER ELEMENT IN THE HOME

Water is traditionally associated with black and dark blue, but I expand this connection to include any blue color that reminds me of natural bodies of water. I have a Caribbean blue-green on my home office walls, tapping into the Water Element that nourishes my Wood and my creative potential.

Water doesn't have a definite shape; it is molded by the container. Water in its natural state is flowing, so shapes that mimic water are undulating curves and irregular patterns, including paisleys.

Water can also be represented by fish, shells, coral, and beach glass. Symbols also include the material of glass and mirrors, which are reflective surfaces. Artwork that incorporates a water or moon theme evokes Water, as well as artwork that is irregular or abstract.

Water Is Deep and Introverted

Water Element is present in the spaces in your home that represent stillness and yin. They are the quiet spaces. Make sure that you have at least one or two quiet spaces for rest and contemplation, such as a treasured meditation room or corner, a great reading nook, or a study.

Perhaps you have a long unoccupied child's room that's now an occasional guest room in your home. Consider making this a special private space just for you. Create a small altar for meditation with a cozy chair and lamp for journaling and reading. Do your daily morning yoga routine. Decorate it with the essence of the Water Element, both calming and nurturing to your soul.

In our homes, our bedrooms should be the most yin of all spaces. This will support proper rest and rejuvenation. Keeping your bedroom electronics- and clutter-free is a great start to creating a calming space.

Water Is Imaginative and Playful

Does your home have unusual or playful nooks and crannies? This is the Water Element: unexpected and imaginative. Incorporate a sense of whimsy and fun to inspire creativity through funny sayings, children's drawings, or interesting artwork.

One of the things I love about my current home is its whimsy. There are two stairways to the basement and my children loved to run up and down, chasing each other. We had a large kitchen cabinet that connected the dining room and kitchen (a great hiding place and escape hatch) and tiny "elf-size" doors that open into the roof eaves for added storage in the bedrooms upstairs. The house was full of charm and fun for our young family!

Water Is Calm and Flowing

The most powerful way to activate the Water Element in your home is with real water—installing a water fountain, an aquarium, or even a bowl of Water (as long as you change the water every few days) is great. Moving, clean water is associated with life and vitality. It is also connected to abundance and money.

If you are lucky enough to have water views, maximize them in your home with limited window treatments to take advantage of the vista. I also suggest placement of a mirror to reflect a beautiful water view into your home. In addition, the sound of water, as ocean waves, rain, or a trickling stream, is a wonderful way to tap into the Water Element in your home. (But note, that a leaky faucet does *not* serve this purpose!)

THE WATER ELEMENT IN THE GARDEN

Water in the garden is so natural. Water nourishes the trees, plants, and flowers on our property, so we often have sprinklers to play this role. And another common water feature in the suburbs is the pool. Spending time in a pool provides a cooling respite to the hot summer sun. It is playful and often reminds us of childhood.

If you are lucky enough to have a natural body of water on your property, this is a bonus as it pertains to feng shui. Water is half of the term *feng shui*, which means "wind and water." Water brings yang energy (life) and vitality to the land.

However, if you do not have natural water features, artificial ponds and waterfalls are a wonderful addition to a yard. The movement of water increases its life-giving properties. Be sure that you position a waterfall to flow *toward* rather than *away from* your home, as it will direct the life-giving properties your way.

A hot tub is another way to bring the properties of water into your space. The heat of the tub also creates Fire energy and, with it, intimacy and togetherness.

THE WATER ELEMENT IN NATURE

In early times, bodies of water provided ease of transportation. In fact, only 150 years ago, local villagers boated over to the shore of Connecticut from Long Island's North Shore to make their purchases, rather than travel the fifteen miles or so to the South Shore!

Now, roads and pathways function as our main transportation. On land paths provide the conduit for the flow of people and chi. Sometimes, I find that clients neglect this aspect of a pleasing home. Be sure you have a sufficient pathway to your front door, and if possible, make it a curved path, so the chi can gently meander and not push aggressively through a straight, direct route.

Roadways help transport our cars, especially in the suburbs. If you live in a neighborhood with a tangle of roads, this creates confusion for visitors as well as for chi. Your home will not receive its full abundance of chi. If this is the case for you, the land will be very yin. So adding movement and vitality (Fire) to your property will attract chi—objects such as lighting, wind chimes, moving whirligigs, and, of course, flowing water features work very well.

Conversely, if your home is on a very busy road, build up protection against this rushing, aggressive chi, preferably with landscaping or fencing.

As mentioned before, if you live near a natural body of water, this can be very auspicious. Water that is gentle and meandering is best. If the movement is very rigorous, as with ocean waves, it can threaten and destroy your home and your luck. Cure this very yang land with some added yin, such as landscaping and rocks. If the water is stagnant (yin), filling only with rain and having no underground spring feeding it—known as a "kettle hole" (with no underground source)—it can contribute to negative energy and poor luck. Add more yang energy by placing some lighting or movement such as a waterfall.

There are many ways we can connect with the Water Element.

You can swim in a natural water source, such as a deep lake, the rolling ocean, or a lazy river. Immerse yourself in the raging power of a waterfall. Even standing inside one can be a wonderful experience. You could also visit a grand one, like Niagara.

Listening to the sounds of water, such as ocean waves, the ripples of a lake, or even an artificial waterfall or fountain or just viewing water in an aquarium or even a water-themed screen saver can provide us the respite we need during our daily lives.

You can take a walk during or after a rainstorm, and breathe in the smell of rain, full of negative ions that are very healing to the body. They help clear the air of mold spores, pollen, bacteria, and viruses, along with other hazardous airborne particles.

You can ponder the full moon every month, which brightens the usual dark sky. You can sit in contemplation in the middle of the night, when it's most quiet and still. This is the time of great access to the spirit, when distractions are at their minimum. Even in winter—the Water Element season—meditation seems easier, as we go within just as nature does.

THE SACRED

DREAMING

How connected are you to your dreams? Everyone dreams to some extent, but being aware of your dreams in a more conscious way often does require some work on your part. You do need to make an intention to recall your dreams and give yourself some space to manifest that in your life. Being aware of the messages from our dreams is an important aspect of spiritual growth.

Our dreams provide us with symbols or, sometimes, actual images of where we are in our everyday lives—often helping us with mundane issues, such as getting a new job, as well as higher spiritual issues. Dreams can provide us with a status on where we are with our spiritual growth. If you'd like to connect with the Water Element in your life, taking time to reflect on your dreams is a great way to do this.

DREAM JOURNALING EXERCISE

For most people, remembering their dreams seems challenging. The symbols from dreams seem to vanish like snowflakes melting through our minds as we rise and start our day. Here are a few tips to help you start your dream work in earnest, if you so choose:

Keep a journal and pen by the side of your bed. Even a piece of paper will suffice. Upon lying down, say to yourself that you intend to remember your dreams in the morning. If you have a particular life issue you would like assistance with, ask for guidance about it. This can be anything from a simple request about handling a minor problem at work or as big as how you should manage a specific relationship in your life. Keep an open mind and assume that you will receive advice.

It may be that you'll receive a message that night or it may take a few nights. So keep at it every night.

If you awake during the course of your night, notice if you can recall anything from your dreams. Jot them down, even if it's just a few words that may spark your memory the next morning. One great tip that works for me is to actually title the dream (such as "Falling Down a Waterfall") or even just note one significant symbol from the dream (such as "a gold cylinder").

Create a morning ritual where you are able to write down as much as you can about your dreams in a journal or notebook. Date and title them. As soon as you can, spend some time thinking about the major symbols and actions taken in the dream. How did you feel in the dream and when you awoke? Were there a series of small, seemingly unrelated "dreamlettes"? Perhaps they are all related to your question, such as showing you do this and then this happens, then you do that, etc. Any words actually spoken or read (most communication is telepathic) are extremely important.

After you consider what the dream means, if you still need assistance working with the symbols in the dream, check out a dream dictionary for potential answers.

As I've said, dreams have been extremely important in my spiritual life. They have helped me make the right decisions, follow the right path, and have provided a positive, empowering perspective over challenges in my life. They will never steer you wrong. Besides meditation, dream work has been the single most effective tool for me since follow-ing a more spiritual path.

PURIFYING BATH MEDITATION

Both the Celts and the Japanese acknowledged the power of waterfalls in purification. The Japanese Shinto practice of *misogi* is an intense rite that uses a combination of prayer, breathing, exercise, and immersion into a waterfall for purification and renewal.

A more readily available ritual is this Purifying Bath Meditation. Draw a bath with a temperature that is right for you. Before stepping in, ask the Water to cleanse, heal, purify, and remove negative energy, whether it be physical, emotional, mental, or spiritual.

Once in the Water, ask the Water for a message about your physi-cal, emotional, or spiritual pain. Be open to receiving images, words, or colors that can help you to express your pain verbally. If you do not receive a message, just know that you are being healed and you may receive a message later on (or even during a dream). Before exiting the tub, give thanks for the purification. You can also do this meditation in the shower.

CASE STUDIES

Lisa Lacks a Path

A few years ago, Lisa called me to help her enhance business. She is a health coach who works out of a home office and said that she felt somewhat stuck and unproductive. She also hoped to increase her client list and stimulate referrals. Lisa has a warm, enthusiastic per-sonality. She's a go-getter and always looking for new approaches and perspectives to help her clients with the often-challenging con-cept of sticking to a healthy lifestyle and diet. Lisa is on the cutting edge of nutrition counseling. A thought-leader with great ambi-tion, she confided to me that she was a bit of a workaholic. She found that she neglected her personal life and relationships a bit.

It was not surprising that Lisa's primary True Nature Element is Wood.

Upon reviewing her property, I found that she was fortunate to have an outbuilding that served as the perfect office space. On her wide lot, the office was diagonally opposite her home, probably a hundred feet from the house.

I asked her how clients typically walked to her office, observing that there was not a path to follow. She explained that they walked across her grass. Prospective clients literally didn't have a path to her business. The positive intention of creating a route to her office was not lost on her. I suggested that she lay a path of inexpensive pieces of slate in a curved design across the lawn. She was exhilarated at the idea and had it installed just a few short weeks after our consultation.

To help her with a bit of Wood imbalance, I suggested that she bring both the Water Element (supports Wood) and the Wood Element into her home office and bedroom.

She added a water fountain in her home office to not only support her Wood, but also to attract business prospects since in feng shui moving water represents opportunity and abundance. She added several plants that not only looked good in the space, but also refreshed the air and removed toxins from her computer equipment that builds up in the small room. We repositioned her desk so that she had good placement and a view of the office doorway and allowed her to see the beautiful trees and garden outside her window to support her Wood Element.

In her bedroom, Lisa loved the idea of nourishing her Wood Element by painting the walls a soft sage green. She also changed out her bedding with paisley (a Water Element pattern) linens. She already had a beautiful photo of the ocean that she loved from her travels so we positioned it directly across from her bed so that she saw it first upon waking. I also suggested she do some dream work for guidance on her business. Lisa took my recommendations to heart.

As a result of these changes, Lisa saw a boom in business opportunities and strategic partnerships. It has also given her a more balanced perspective in her life, managing to take time for her relationships with family and friends.

Diane's Descent into the Yin

Diane retired from a career of several decades due to debilitating illness. She was in her early sixties and not feeling ready for retirement. She had been a successful manager in a well-paying job and was respected in her role as a leader of a team when she was diagnosed with Raynaud's disease. Raynaud's attacks the circulatory system and creates extreme bouts of coldness in the arms and legs. After she went several months in and out of work, it was determined that it would be best for her to "medically retire" from her job. Although she loved her work, she just didn't have the energy it required anymore. In fact, some days the pain was so bad that she didn't get out of bed.

Diane explained that she was sharing her home with her daughter and her daughter's family. To make room for her grandsons, she had moved into the smaller part of the house. When I toured the house with Diane and her daughter, I saw that her side of the house was about two feet lower than the rest and on the concrete foundation. This area was the converted garage.

During our discussion, I saw that both Diane and her daughter were very intuitive and connected with energy. They both said that the energy in the house was chaotic and lacked harmony. Diane said further that the energy in her home was all "illness and stale."

Diane told me that while working, she had been energetic, "alive and vibrant; now, I'm not." She had socialized a lot with her co-workers, loved her work, and now she rarely left the house. Not long ago, she had also been open to alternative therapies and did deep inner work, neither of which she continued. When I asked her why, she didn't have an answer. I asked about dreaming, and she said that because of her illness she often had trouble sleeping. She had to take medication to get any rest, "so I don't dream anymore." She also no longer enjoyed any hobbies; her only joys were her grandsons.

Although Diane had a fair amount of the Wood Element in her ambition and motivation in her career, I saw that her True Nature was Water. But at some point her Water Element had become imbalanced. It could be that her Wood Element became unbalanced first perhaps many years earlier when as a single working mother, she had been striving to do it all. On a physical level, she perhaps didn't allow herself time to rest and replenish (Water), so her Wood collapsed. And then the Water Element became overactive.

The Water Element represents winter and midnight—cold, dark and still. The relationship of excess Water to her illness was striking.

When I mentioned to her that Water is creative, she lit up for the first time in our discussion. That struck a deep, resonating chord within her. She said, "Yes, I was so creative! I loved to paint!"

Diane's environment contributed to a drop into "still" Water. Diane's "sunken" space on a concrete slab only added to the yin quality of her life situation. The cold she experienced was extreme yin, extreme Water in excess. The clutter in the house, mostly from the grandchildren, contributed to a feeling of chaos. The energy in the home did indeed feel inharmonious due to the challenges of sharing a space with extended family. In short, Diane had too much yin, too much Water, and was living in a depressed state. She needed to find her way out of this, if she was up to the task.

To get her stagnant Water moving, I recommended a water fountain in her private space. To uplift the overwhelming yin quality, I suggested adding some warmth with an electric fireplace (opposite her bed so as not to expose her to high electromagnetic fields), and with colorful area rugs and some bright artwork that inspired her— perhaps her own! In fact, to spark passion in her, I recommended that she start painting again or taking up any other creative activity that inspired her. In a space clearing and blessing ceremony, we set the intention of raising her side of the house symbolically, to make her side equal with the rest of the house and, therefore, equal in relationship. We added several live, healthy plants to raise the chi as well as a weekly bouquet of flowers (nothing says joy like fresh flowers!).

REFRESH YOUR WATER POWER!

Too much Water is like a tidal wave moving across the land, creating destruction with its cynicism, suspicion, and tactlessness. It causes people to run! Too little Water is like a dried up creek, overwhelmed with fear and doubt, detracting from the joy of life.

Balanced Water is refreshing and exciting. She is artistic and shares her gifts with all. She reminds us that inner reflection and self-awareness are key to being a whole, healthy person. Water shows us how to slow down, rest, and be in the moment. Water brings the imagination and capacity to incubate ideas, waiting to emerge from the ground when the timing is right. Water is playful and creative, although deep and mysterious. She refreshes us with life and provides the space for chi to flow.

To reclaim your Water power, you can wear clothing that represents Water, such as flowing skirts and loose chiffon tops. Dark colors such as black and blue, as well as eclectic, retro outfits from the vintage store. Handmade and one-of-a kind fashion and glass-beaded jewelry are Water.

You can practice daily quiet time for reflection—even ten minutes is a great start. Slow down and schedule some time to nurture yourself. If your well runs dry, how can you nourish the village? Connect with Water in nature through sensual baths or a swim in the ocean. Add a lively water fountain to your home office or by your front door to allow the chi to flow smoothly throughout your home. Create pathways and be sure that pathways are clear of obstructions. Hang a water scene across from your favorite chair. Paint your walls Caribbean blue! Keep a dream journal and nourish your deep soulful self. Pay attention to the signs and symbols connecting you with the other dimensions of our reality.

PART THREE

Creating
Luminous Spaces

*Wonderful how completely everything in wild nature fits into
us, as if truly part and parent of us. The sun shines not on us
but in us. The rivers flow not past, but through us, thrilling,
tingling, vibrating every fiber and cell of the substance of our
bodies, making them glide and sing. The trees wave and the
flowers bloom in our bodies as well as our souls, and every
bird song, wind song, and; tremendous storm song of the rocks
in the heart of the mountains is our song, our very own, and
sings our love.*

— John Muir, "Mountain Thoughts"

In this last section of the book, you will discover the element that
represents your True Nature. You will learn what physical, emotional, and spiritual qualities define you and how you can bring
your True Nature Element's qualities in your home and your life.

Learning about the Elements and their connection to nature helps
us create spaces that are balanced and harmonious and support us.

Having spaces in tune with these natural Elements allows us to sink into and own our True Nature, acknowledge our strengths and weaknesses, and explore our authentic selves, our gifts.

These Elements gives us the ability to learn not only what makes us tick, but also what motivates those closest to us. We surely have seen qualities of the Elements in our parents, siblings, partner, children, and friends. We notice predominant strengths and weaknesses within ourselves and them. The qualities of the Five Elements are archetypes that show up regardless of class, race, culture, or gender. These archetypes are alive within the patterns of the soul of humanity throughout the span of time. They provide us with a window into ourselves and others, and in the process of learning, we will hopefully come to understand our relationships from a more loving, compassionate place.

Chapter 10

What Is Your True Nature?

The forces that move the cosmos are no different from those which move the human soul.

—Lama Anagarika Govinda

Understanding these Five Element archetypes helps us take a fresh look at nature's positive influence on our health and well-being. It shows how nature can stimulate the relaxation response and improve our lives. This wisdom has been used to restore health for thousands of years when applied in Traditional Chinese Medicine. We can share in this wisdom by bringing in the energy of the Five Elements into our inner and outer spaces.

Our homes can be spaces of light and with our conscious attention we can tap into this energy for personal power by understanding our unique elemental makeup. With the results from the True Nature Assessments that follow, you will understand how you can incorporate the qualities of nature in your home based on your own unique needs. Knowing how the Elements impact your life means you can raise your personal power, energy, and consciousness.

UNDERSTANDING WHO YOU ARE

Who are you? You might answer by telling me about your career, your marital status, your education, where you live, or your family history. But these are exterior factors based on your circumstances. *How did you get where you are?* What is your motivating force? What are your desires in life? What are your goals, but more importantly, *why* are these your goals? Your genetics, your experiences, your circumstances, and free will contribute to who you are and who you will become. *What is the underlying fabric of you?*

We each have a unifying force or archetype that is predominant throughout our life. It helps us navigate the world, provides a foundation for our sense of identity, and helps us set goals for what we need to be satisfied in life. If we are not connected with that unifying identity, we feel dissonance in our lives; we lack true joy, we experience negative emotions or feel that we are not being the best we can be. We may be trying to live up to someone else's idea of who we should be and always falling short. If we aren't connected with our core being, we will have low self-esteem and won't know what we want or need in life.

If we are not connected, our energy and consciousness will have limited or no development. We will not see how our words, thoughts, or actions impacted our life and got us to where we are today. We may blame others for our circumstances. We may lack a feeling of true power and settle for the role of the victim or the perpetrator, acting from a need for self-preservation. Everything we experience in life will be seen through this lens of powerlessness. This consciousness lacks self-awareness and responsibility and doesn't recognize that our actions create our own reality.

This inner imbalance is reinforced by a cultural imbalance, in what Theodore Roszak, the father of ecopsychology, calls "despair of the soul." In our society most of the natural elements have been polluted, exaggerated, diminished, or weakened. The Earth has been disrespected and dishonored. We have disrupted the natural balance and harmony of the processes of our world, and this distortion is reflected in our distorted consciousness. We are not only in disharmony with the *Earth*, but we are in disharmony within *ourselves*.

But we can reengage and ignite our power by learning our True Nature and connecting with it in an intimate ongoing way.

You can regain the clarity of the Elements in their true form, connecting with your True Nature and aligning with its energy in your home and your life. Once you do that, your unique gifts and talents can blossom. You will truly be able to express its archetypal energy. Your light will be rekindled, and you will live with joy, passion, and enthusiasm for your unique self.

WHAT ELEMENT AM I?

To discover your True Nature Element, take the What Is Your True Nature? Assessments covering three different formats. You may choose to do one, two, or all three. Here is an overview:

Part one contains an eighteen-question quiz. The questions cover your preferences, your motivations, and how you live your life or how you wish you could live your life.

Part two is a descriptor list. By consulting your journal or going back to the Element chapters, see what words you highlighted to determine what Element really resonated with you. Journal anything that arises about what Element you feel you identify with. Once you are finished, you can count up the words on the list and add them to the Summary of Results Chart at the end. Or you may prefer to use Chart 1: Attributes of the Five Elements in the Appendix and circle those words you resonate with.

Part three is a reflection exercise. A series of open-ended questions about your childhood and major, and even, minor life choices and how the Elements played a role in those times of your life will refine and clarify for you how you tend to operate and which Element you most identify with.

Tips—Here are a few important things to keep in mind:

- As you go through each question in part one and rate each response, feel each response in your gut. Don't think about it much. Usually our first reactions are truer than when we let our minds ponder a response!
- You might feel drawn to rate two responses with a "4" for the same question. That's okay. In fact, the top two responses usually paint a clearer picture of you than just the "best" answer.
- If you don't understand or feel moved to respond to a particular question, skip it.
- Your True Nature motives and desires may be partially unconscious. That is why I have included space for reflection, so that you can think about actual decisions you have made in your life and what motivated you. Sometimes we may not want to admit to what we see as a flaw or imperfection. Be aware that you don't pick what you wish your response could be. Do not deceive yourself or allow your ego to deceive you. There is nothing to gain by typing yourself as an Element that is not you. (These Assessments are available on my website, *luminous-spaces.com*, as a PDF download. Just enter your information and get access to other free bonuses!)

WHAT IS YOUR TRUE NATURE? ASSESSMENTS

Part One: Quiz

Place the score for each Element in the "Summary of Results Chart" at end of this chapter.

What is Your True Nature? Part 1

Directions: For each question below, rate each possible response with a score: 0 = Not me at all!   1 = Sometimes 3 = Often   4 = Definitely me! (There is no "2.")

1. Best describes my work ethic:

____ Wood   I am ambitious

____ Fire   I am a good worker, but look forward to TGIF!

____ Earth   I would rather tend to home affairs if I could

____ Metal   I am punctual; follow rules and procedures

____ Water   I prefer to freelance; not to have set work times

2. Best describes how I work with others:

____ Wood   I often lead/have difficulty following others

____ Fire   I love collaborating with others

____ Earth   I prefer to be in the background

____ Metal   I am a natural leader

____ Water   I prefer to work alone

3. How I respond to change:

____ Wood   I find excitement navigating through it

____ Fire   I love the adventure of possibilities

____ Earth   I prefer things to stay the same

____ Metal   I often feel uneasy with change. I like control

____ Water   I go with the flow

4. My communication style:

____ Wood   I am assertive

____ Fire   I am sensitive

____ Earth   I am nurturing

____ Metal   I am logical

____ Water   I often don't share my opinions

5. How I respond to projects:

____ Wood   I'm great at starting new projects

____ Fire   lots of enthusiasm to start, but it dissipates quickly

____ Earth   great at getting consensus from others

____ Metal   I create a schedule and list of to-do's right away

____ Water   I often uncover great insight for improvements

6. My talent is . . .

___ Wood   coordinating
___ Fire   lighting the way for others
___ Earth   negotiating
___ Metal   creating structure
___ Water   my imagination

7. I'm often absorbed with . . .

___ Wood   new projects
___ Fire   pleasure
___ Earth   peace at all costs
___ Metal   strict adherence to rules
___ Water   self-discovery

8. A word that describes me is . . .

___ Wood   adventurous
___ Fire   humorous
___ Earth   diplomatic
___ Metal   high integrity
___ Water   calm

9. Another word that describes me:

___ Wood   confident
___ Fire   romantic
___ Earth   maternal
___ Metal   perfectionist
___ Water   honest

10. My emotional tendency is . . .

___ Wood   anger and/or frustration
___ Fire   anxiety
___ Earth   worry
___ Metal   grief
___ Water   fear

11. When I get stressed I usually feel . . .
___ Wood   exasperated or blame others
___ Fire   scattered and/or panicky
___ Earth   emotional
___ Metal   critical and/or detached
___ Water   hopeless and/or internalize

12. My preferred weekend activity is . . .
___ Wood   do something new and/or adventurous
___ Fire   out having fun with friends/partner
___ Earth   spend quiet time with a good friend/partner
___ Metal   attend a museum or art event
___ Water   work quietly on a project or attend a workshop

13. My preferred clothing is . . .
___ Wood   business casual, sporty
___ Fire   bright, bold, animal prints
___ Earth   comfortable, classic pieces
___ Metal   sharp, sophisticated, designer clothes
___ Water   eclectic and/or flowing, loose

14. My feelings around clutter:
___ Wood   I have some clutter, but I'm too busy now
___ Fire   I have lots of unfinished projects in my home
___ Earth   I don't have clutter—my home is filled with great memories/collections
___ Metal   I hate clutter! I cannot feel comfortable.
___ Water   you may call this clutter, but it feeds my soul

15. My "way of being" is . . .
___ Wood   pushing forward
___ Fire   all over
___ Earth   stable
___ Metal   reducing, filtering
___ Water   still, observing

16. For balance of my energy, I require . . .
___ Wood   moments of stillness
___ Fire   coolness
___ Earth   movement, activity
___ Metal   flexibility
___ Water   warmth/heat

17. My emotional fear is . . .
___ Wood   to lose my freedom
___ Fire   to be left out
___ Earth   to be not needed
___ Metal   to lose integrity
___ Water   to be exposed

18. My dream career is . . .
___ Wood   successful entrepreneur or explorer
___ Fire   keynote speaker or performer
___ Earth   taking care, advocating for others
___ Metal   CEO, design, justice
___ Water   therapist, artist, musician, writer

Part Two: Descriptors

Review what you highlighted in the Element chapters (i.e., enthusiastic in the Fire chapter or competitive in the Wood chapter). Write those words in the chart below or your journal. Or if you prefer, refer to chart 1 in the appendix and circle the ones that you resonate with there:

Wood	Fire	Earth	Metal	Water

Count how many words describing each Element resonated with you and place these numbers in the Summary of Results Chart at end of this chapter.

Part Three: Reflection

This section requires you to take some time and space to read through each question, contemplate your responses, and record them here or in a journal.

When you are ready, rate each Element for each question using the scale of 0-4 ("2" is purposely missing to get a clearer result.):

0 = Not me at all!
1 = Sometimes
3 = Often
4 = Definitely me!

Once you are finished rating the responses to each question, place the scores in the "Summary of Results Chart" at the end of this chapter.

1. Childhood Element

In our childhoods, our authentic selves usually show through very early. Is there one Element that you identified with as a child? For instance: Were you the class clown (Fire)? Did you like to play quietly by yourself (Water)? Did you keep your bedroom very organized and neat (Metal)?

Did you journal about any memories that came to you while reading through the Element chapters? If so, consider your reactions and emotions to those situations. Perhaps your family said things about you that described aspects of you (i.e., "No grass grows under her feet!"). What Element(s) seem to resonate with you from those memories as a child?

___ exploring, always trying new things, rebellious (Wood)
___ extrovert, often the center of attention (Fire)
___ caring for others and helping them get along (Earth)
___ more interested in studies, doing things right (Metal)
___ introvert, inventing, wild imagination (Water)

Are the qualities of the Element that resonated most with you as a child still strong within you now? If not, why not? That Element was probably an expression of your authentic self before you were influenced by others. What influenced you to focus on a different Element? Was it something or someone in your life? Perhaps you were influenced to develop an important secondary Element that is still with you today?

For instance, I was Wood and Fire as a child, but after the death of my father when I was eleven years old, I started developing the Water Element (philosophy and meaning of life) and now I see it as an important secondary Element in my life. As I mentioned in the Water Element chapter, I cultivated a keen fascination with and interest in philosophy, psychology, and metaphysics that has only deepened as I've gotten older.

2. Driving Motivation

Consider the big events in your life. What was behind your motivation to do what you chose to do? Some suggestions could be your decision to select a major in college, the career you are currently in, why you did or didn't take that promotion, or why or where you decided to move. Consider a romantic relationship in your life, if the driving motive wasn't that you fell in love. Consider a few smaller choices, like your hobbies, where you (or would like to) travel, or doing something new in your life.

Write down a brief synopsis of each situation and your feelings about it now and then. Did you listen to your inner voice or the voice of others?

For instance, my decision to change my career path was driven by a deep need to have meaning in my life and to seek truth and knowledge. As is common for those in midlife, my powerful Water Element motivations rose up.

_____

_____

_____

_____

_____

_____

Now ask yourself what was really behind your motivation to do what you chose to do. Take some time and space to reflect on this. Go deeper. Sometimes there is a surface motivation that we believe is correct, but often something deeper was really the driver. Sometimes we don't want to admit our true motivations. Be honest. That is the only way you can truly learn about yourself. Which *one* of these motivations was **at the heart** of most of your decisions in life? (Read through the list by Element of motivations below. Write "4" next to your primary motivation and "3" next to any secondary motivation.)

___ To win, have power, sense of adventure, to be unique, be independent (Wood)

___ To be adored, in the spotlight, for pleasure, crave excitement, crave change (Fire)

___ To help others, please others, have stability, be responsible, avoid conflict (Earth)

___ A logical choice, to have the finer things, the ethical/moral choice, respect for authority (Metal)

___ To be safe, to have meaning, to be self-sufficient, seek truth/ knowledge, went with the flow, just fell into it (Water)

3. Personal Stories

Perhaps some of the personal stories shared in this book triggered a memory or two. Write a brief synopsis of that memory. What Element does it correspond with?

_____

_____

_____

_____

4. Nature Memory

Think about at least one standout experience that you had in nature (or two or three). Write a bit about the location, what you experienced, and what made it so important for you.

For instance, a standout memory for me was on a cross-country trip to Utah and Arizona. We experienced abundant nighttime thunderstorms and turbulent weather along with beautiful days. Watching the big changing skies and observing the weather was a significant experience for me, which symbolizes the Metal Element.

_____

_____

_____

_____

_____

_____

_____

Select which Element best represents that experience. Write "4" next to that one:

___ Trees, plants or flowers, camping, forest, woods (Wood)

___ Sun, summer at the beach, desert, lightning, fire (Fire)

___ Mountains, soil, stone, or open landscape (Earth)

___ Wind, breezes, tornadoes, hurricanes, storms, looking at the night sky (Metal)

___ Natural body of water, floods, snow, rain (Water)

Summary of Results Chart

In the chart below, write your scores from each of the assessments and total up each column.

	Wood	Fire	Earth	Metal	Water
Quiz 1					
Quiz 2					
Quiz 3					
1- Childhood					
2 – Driving Motivation*					
3-Stories					
4-Nature					
TOTAL					

*There are several rows to record the multiple experiences you reviewed.

What Element stands out? _____

Is there a secondary Element? _____

Do these Elements make sense to you?

_____

_____

_____

_____

_____

_____

_____

_____

_____

You may find that there are two Elements that are tied or close. If so, then you have two True Nature Elements. When you read through the Elements chapters again, you might find that you resonate with one more than the other.

If there are two Elements that are very close in score, ask for a sign or symbol to show itself to you today in a way that you will understand the message clearly. For instance, if you were balanced between Metal and Water and a friend just called you out of the blue to go boating, then I would say the sign is for Water! Watch for anything out of the ordinary.

Go back now to that chapter and see how you resonate with that Element's strengths and weaknesses (or you can refer to chart 2 in the appendix, which lists the strengths and weaknesses of each Element).

When you first read the Element chapters, you may have been drawn to a different Element. Consider which Element feels more you. Remember to be true to yourself and not swayed by a desire to be something you are not! ***Rejoice in the glory of who you are!***

Chapter 11

Creating Your Luminous Spaces

"Our species once had two sources of inspiration and meaning: religion and the universe, the natural world. But we have turned away from nature . . . the great work of the 21st century will be to reconnect to the natural world as a source of meaning."
—Richard Louv, *The Nature Principle*

Most of us realize that we need nature in our daily lives to have a sense of well-being, whether it takes the form of a walk in the woods or mindfully observing the sun, the breezes, and the wildlife outside our windows.

We need to connect with *all* of nature to develop into emotionally and spiritually mature adults, but there is a predominant *quality* from nature that resides in our souls—the seed from which all things in our lives flow. When we bond with that quality in nature, our True Nature Element, we align ourselves—perhaps for the first time in our lives—with our purpose and calling. And we are able to tap into the strengths of that Element, restoring greater balance and harmony in our lives.

By bringing our True Nature Elements into our homes and lives, we are able to create luminous spaces within and without. Luminous spaces are restorative and peaceful. And because our homes are a mirror of our lives, a luminous home will bring balance and peace into our everyday life. We will have greater health and well-being and feel more joy.

As I mentioned in part one of this book, there are three main concepts that we must understand in order to embark on this spiritual journey of our True Natures.

First, we must acknowledge that each being, animated or not, and every space we inhabit have a form of energy and consciousness. We are all interrelated and connected, and our thoughts, words, and actions have a tremendous impact on everyone and everything we come into contact with. If we lived truly conscious of this knowledge on a daily basis, all our lives would be so different!

Second, we must recognize that our homes have a powerful, often subconscious, influence over us. Regardless of the decor or the type of house, it is most important that our homes and their contents resonate with us on a deep soul level. If not, we will live disconnected and fragmented lives, always seeking on the outside what is not nourished inside.

And third, we must consciously "bring the light" into our spaces with the higher vibrations of nature. We need to have mindful awareness of what we bring into our homes and our lives. We need to be conscious of the vibrations of our environment and the people in our lives. We can tap into our intuition, to gauge the life-affirming properties of our homes and objects within. We can use the information I have included here to help restore a deeper connection to nature in our homes.

To bring in the light, we need to connect with our True Nature Element. When we align with our Element, we find balance and harmony. We will naturally leverage the strengths of that Element and address the weaknesses. If there is another Element that we need to bring into harmony, we can incorporate aspects of that Element as well.

Remember, that all of the Five Elements are within each of us. They all play a role in how we move through our lives. Wood gives us the ability to start new projects; Fire sparks connection with others; Earth provides stability and responsibility; Metal helps us with structure and ethics; and Water gives us space for reflection and individuality.

Although you may not be particularly great at organization and structure, you do have some ability to tap into Metal. Perhaps you want to be able to connect better with your Metal to help with a particular work project. Go through the Metal chapter and see what you can do to bring Metal more prominently into your office space. Perhaps you can declutter and organize your office, as well as hang a beautiful piece of artwork that will inspire you.

While you may procrastinate, you still have the Wood Element within you. If you find that you want to start something new in your life, tap into the power of Wood by making a point to stop and notice the wonderful, magical trees in your daily life. Buy a fresh bouquet and place it in the entry to your home, so you see it every day. Move around your seating so that you have a new view, a new perspective of things.

You might find it hard to forgive others, but you still have the warmth of Fire in you. Practice forgiveness with little things first. Do the Fire Meditation. Bring some red into your bedroom. Light a candle. Get a pet and lavish it with affection. Have a party in your home. These will all help the Fire energy burn more brightly in your heart.

Perhaps you cannot get to sleep at night, but you still have the Water Element in you. Listen to the sounds of water before you go to sleep. Take some time to be still before you go to bed. Practice meditation. Go swimming and feel the luxury of water against your skin. Allow yourself some unstructured time. Schedule it if you have to. Take some time to just be.

Although you bounce from one thing to another, you still have the Earth Element in you. Do the Connecting Heaven and Earth Meditation, which will ground your energy. Carry a smoky quartz crystal in your pocket to create stability. Take a walk on the beach and collect some stones. Place them in a bowl on your desk.

See how the chart below contributes to a smooth flow of energy, from project conception and germination (Water), to the courage of taking those first steps (Wood), to the vision and enthusiasm bringing the project "out there" (Fire), to assembling a team and putting in the hard work (Earth), to the confidence to see the project through with discipline and leadership (Metal). Then Water provides the insight to move onward.

This natural energy moves through our lives in a spiral, just as the seasons. Sometimes we short-circuit that energy when we are not in balance, or perhaps have underdeveloped aspects of ourselves. Sometimes we need help to initiate or to assemble a team. Some of us may lend support with our stability or organization skills. We are all so unique and have our unique gifts that we can lend to others to complete the process. And this is how knowledge of the Five Elements can help us become more whole.

The Five Element Process for Goal Achievement

www.luminous-spaces.com
Re-Nature Consulting, LLC © 2016

DEALING WITH CLUTTER

Another form of negative energy in our homes is clutter. If you are among the many challenged by clutter, or perhaps have a partner that is, I do sympathize with your situation. Many people ask me what they can do to overcome this challenge, which is contributing to negative energy, chaos, and imbalance in their home.

If you consider that our homes are a mirror of our inner spaces, then perhaps we are in this situation because we need to address some level of chaos within ourselves (whether physical, mental, or emotional chaos) or we may simply need to move past this issue that is challenging us to grow.

There is no magic bullet to address clutter. If you are waiting for the big epiphany, I don't have it. What I can offer you is an "inner" solution. This also works when dealing with a partner's or your own anger or depressive tendencies. There is an issue of internal clutter, mental clutter that will create a cloud of low-level energy and consciousness around the home and drag you down. It's real, and we do feel it!

Understanding the behavior behind the clutter can help a great deal. Clutter is often a result of a feeling of lack and scarcity. You or your partner may be missing something on an emotional level. It often flows from childhood and perhaps a parental relationship. One thing is for certain: clutter is blocking energy.

UNDERSTANDING WHAT'S BEHIND THE CLUTTER

One professional organizer says the clutter is "a way that unhappiness expresses itself." Perhaps, if you or your partner is open to it, you can journal your feelings around the clutter. What unhappiness might it be expressing? What situation or relationship in the past does it represent? Is that a healthy connection? If the clutter is blocking something from entering my life, what does it represent? How will I feel when that block is no longer there and great opportunities present themselves? Am I open to that now?

Consider the type of clutter that you have in the home. For instance,

- Sentimental clutter—This represents attachment to things in the past. It may also represent the fear of guilt for getting rid of those objects (Earth Element).
- Project clutter—This represents the inability to finish projects and may be too much Fire or too little Metal (which facilitates completion).
- "Just in case" clutter—This represents the need to keep things "just in case." It's about fearing that you will not have what you need when you need it (Water Element).
- Paper clutter—We keep magazines and article clippings in piles until we can finally read them. (When will that be?) It is a variation on the theme of not having something when you need it. But with the Internet, great information is easily accessible without the buildup of paper (Wood Element).

Identifying your True Nature Element might help you understand what is going on behind this behavior. We might realize that our family are not intentionally trying to make us crazy (if they are, then we might need to rethink this relationship!). The Earth Element has a great affinity to sentimental items (perhaps a thirty-year-old son's baby clothes, a chair that was Aunt Molly's, or dusty old doodads from Grandpa's basement) when out of balance. She often keeps these items out of guilt (how can I get rid of Aunt Molly's chair?) and out of attachment to the loved one.

Messiness can have different motivators. For Wood, it's that he has too many more important things to do. For Fire, it's impulsively jumping from one thing to another once enthusiasm wanes—which happens quickly! Water? Well, Water flows and needs a container, hence things can start spilling out all over the place. Notice that I don't mention Metal? That's because balanced Metal despises clutter and messiness.

Recognize the Issue of Control

We can only control ourselves. We know this; however, we don't always act in concert with that understanding when the clutter is being generated by a loved one. We think that trying to coerce them, yelling louder, or giving an ultimatum will change their behavior. But it doesn't. And we continue to try this tactic even though it doesn't work (didn't Einstein say something about that?). We may finally give up and not say anything more out of frustration, but silence says volumes if our facial expressions, body language, and energy fields are still emanating our disapproval.

So what do we do? It is the hardest and the simplest thing of all: *change our energy about the mess and clutter.* It weighs our energy down and does not let the light grow. I am not suggesting that we *ignore* it. That is not going to work. I'm suggesting that we *acknowledge* it, *but do not lay that heavy anger and frustration onto it.* Raise your consciousness higher and those lower vibrations are less able to reach you. *Let it go.*

We can do some breathing and visualization techniques, as you will read about in chapter seven. We can go out into nature as often as possible. We can do the exercises in this book. We can clear out our own clutter. Sometimes we still have clutter to manage, even if it's not visible. Perhaps it's a closet or our drawers. Perhaps the clutter is in our minds. We might be involved in so many things that we are scattered in our thoughts.

When our energy around this challenge shifts, our loved one will feel it, if only subconsciously. Over time and with a concerted effort on our part, the energy in our home will shift, and their energy will *have to* shift along with it. It is always that way with energy. Everything is interconnected. This may create new openings and opportunities. *Sometimes* the other partner spontaneously clears up. But it all comes back to us.

The trick is that we must be diligent in shifting *our own* energy. This is absolutely the key. We cannot just try this for a week and get discouraged because *the other person* hasn't changed. In just a week, *we* haven't changed either. Modifying our own patterns of behavior and thought requires ongoing work. How long? Think "forever." But it is worth every bit of what we have to gain!

Shift the Energy!

Now that you know your True Nature Element, you can focus your efforts to shift energy on this Element.

Here is what I recommend to help you change the energy in your home to create more luminous spaces:

- First, connect with the consciousness of your home. Do the exercise from chapter two. Learn to open your heart and listen to what your senses and intuition are telling you. Develop a relationship with your home. Recognize its soul and connect to your home in a loving way by giving it gratitude. This is a great start!
- Second, consider your results from the three assessments. If you are torn between two Elements, perhaps ask for a sign or symbol to help you clarify which one should be your focus, or choose to nurture both! Also, you may have identified a different Element that you recognize you are weak in.
- Third, focus your efforts on the one or two Elements to incorporate into your home and life. (You can refer to chart 3 in the appendix for a summary of ways to connect with each of the Elements).

Each Element chapter provided personality characteristics, qualities of the Element in nature, the chi energy of that Element, as well as ideas on how to incorporate that Element into your home and sacred space.

The Archetype Characteristics—Go to the appendix for a list of qualities and characteristics for each of the Five Elements and observe and reflect on these strengths and weaknesses as they arise within you in your daily life—your words, thoughts, and actions. Keep a journal on them. Noticing these qualities in your life will help you forge a stronger bond within yourself and overcome the weaknesses while replacing them with the positive qualities.

In Your Home—Observe your home environment and focus your efforts first on your bedroom, home office, and any place you spend a lot of time (perhaps a living room or porch). The spaces where you pass the majority of your time will have the most influence on you. Look at your space with fresh "feng shui" eyes. Is your True Nature Element represented in your rooms? In your garden? How can you bring more of it in? See what aspects of that Element resonated with you, perhaps using the color, material, or artwork associated with that Element.

Engage in Nature—Make it a point to be out in nature and experience your True Nature Element. Even though you've probably done this before, there is small chance that you did it with a conscious intention to engage in the qualities of that Element. Record your experiences in your journal. Be aware of the signs and signals that nature provides to those who are *observing*. Life is conscious and synchronistic. There are always messages for those paying attention.

The Sacred—Some of the exercises given in this book for connecting to the sacred are in nature and some are in your home. They are instrumental in connecting with the divine energy behind and above all. I have participated in all of these exercises and recommend that you eventually do all of them— particularly those that call to you.

Here's an example of how you might implement this material: You may have learned that your Element is Fire. Add some touches of the Fire Element (see the chart in the appendix) to your bedroom. You might put a few red throw pillows on your bed and place a few candles on your nightstand. You could also hang a picture of a sunrise on the wall. These symbols will enhance your connection to Fire.

In your home office, you might want to reposition your desk so that you have more access to sunlight while you work there. However, be sure that you are in the prospect/refuge or command position, which is important for everyone. You might want to re-paint your office a bold color that you love or open the windows frequently to improve energy and vitality of the room with fresh airflow. You might also add a vase of red flowers to your desk or a faux leopard print pillow to your chair.

To engage with Fire, you may have a nighttime outdoor party to enjoy your fire pit connecting you to both a community and Fire. Add highlights of red flowers to your garden and some star-shaped lights strung around your patio. You may go to the beach and enjoy consciously soaking up Fire energy. You may set aside one evening to do the Fire Meditation on page 106 and record your experiences in your journal as you go through this process.

OTHER WAYS TO SUPPORT YOUR TRUE NATURE ELEMENT

As I mentioned in chapter four, the Five Elements have relationships to one another that are creative (the parent), controlling (grandparent), or draining (child). These relationships are the key to keeping everything in a dynamic tension in the natural world and in balance and harmony in our lives.

Now that you have discovered your True Nature Element, you are not limited to just working with that Element. You can figure in the Creative Element that nourishes your True Nature as well.

Review the chart below and the relationships of your True Nature Element. Then refer back to the chapter that discusses the nourishing Creative Element for ways you can incorporate that Element into your primary spaces like your bedroom, living room, and home office.

For instance, my True Nature Elements are Wood and Fire. I have touches of the Water Element in our bedroom (creates the Wood Element), including deep blue walls, a mirror, a bowl of beach glass (my favorite!), and a beautiful painting of a sailboat on a calm bay. I also have a couple of plants and some dried bamboo stalks (Wood, which supports Fire) and sconces with candles (Fire). I make it a habit to take a walk by the harbor front in my town several times a week and have a regular soak in my deep tub. The trees on my property have a special place in my heart, so I make sure to connect with them and communicate my gratitude. I also make sure that there isn't too much Metal in my spaces, which limits (controls) the Wood energy in my environment. (Refer to chart 3 in the appendix for ideas).

Cycles	Wood True Nature	Fire True Nature	Earth True Nature	Metal True Nature	Water True Nature
Supports	Wood	Fire	Earth	Metal	Water
Creates	Water	Wood	Fire	Earth	Metal
Controls	Metal	Water	Wood	Fire	Earth
Drains	Fire	Earth	Metal	Water	Wood

If your True Nature is Fire, look to both the Wood and Fire Element chapters for inspiration. Some examples would be to add a piece of driftwood into a vignette on your coffee table, hang a few botanical prints in your bedroom, or use flower-adorned bedding. You can add a few red pillows or a purple throw to your sofa and hang a star-shaped light fixture in your living room. Try to watch the sunrise every so often and be truly mindful of the colors of the sky as dawn beckons. Be sure not to have too much Water in your personal spaces, which will control the Fire Element.

If your True Nature is Earth, you can incorporate both Fire and Earth to your home. Throw a few leopard-patterned pillows on your favorite chair or adopt a pet to bring the vitality of the Fire Element into your home. Position yourself to take advantage of the sun during your daily activities. Build a fire pit in your backyard to share with loved ones. Add a stone bench next to the fire pit, place a ceramic bowl filled with some stones you've collected on a walk on your desk, or paint your bedroom walls a beautiful terracotta color. Establish a ritual of lighting some grounding incense, like palo santo, in your home. Practice dowsing on your property to connect with the energy of the earth. Watch the amount of Wood you have in your space. Make sure it's all balanced.

If your True Nature is Metal, you will want to add some Earth and Metal to your decor. Hang a painting with strong mountains to symbolize the grounding and solidity of the Earth Element. Get a side table with a stone top, such as ceramic or slate, to place next to your sofa. Arrange a grouping of square-framed photographs in your entryway. Use wrought-iron seating on your back deck along with a white metal trellis in the garden. Create an archway in a prominent doorway in your home. Adorn your bed with a crisp white comforter and allow the fresh breezes to sweep the air in your home on a daily basis. Be aware not to have too much Fire in your private spaces.

If your True Nature is Water, the Elements of Metal and Water are nurturing for you. You might want to edit down or organize a bookshelf. Place a marble-topped table and a round mirror in your foyer. My very favorite thing to suggest to a Water person is to add a water fountain to one of your public rooms (not your bedroom or you might have to frequent the bathroom during the night!).

Moving water refreshes the air with movement and moisture and the sound is so calming. Touches of black, such as a black cabinet or throw rug or artwork with an ocean or lake scene are great for your living room. Make sure that the Fire Element is not too overbearing in your private spaces.

Another important thing to keep in mind is not having *too much* of an Element that either Controls or Drains your True Nature Element or the Element that your Element controls. Remember Barbara in chapter five? Her True Nature is Fire, but her bedroom had a lot of Metal in it. The bedroom walls, area rugs, window treatments, and bedding were the colors of Metal, and there were several pieces of art that symbolizes the Metal Element. Metal is controlled by Fire, so Metal exhausts the energy of Fire. Wood creates and supports Fire. For balance, Barbara incorporated both Wood and Fire to her space.

IGNITE YOUR PERSONAL POWER!

Hopefully this book has offered you some good insights into how to make your life more joyous and in harmony with the universe. But, we are all different, so our approaches will vary as well.

You will proceed in your own unique way according to your True Nature Element.

The Wood Element

If you are Wood, you are probably psyched about creating exciting possibilities in your life. You are probably very motivated to see change and to start right now—if you haven't already! Perhaps create a list to follow as a reminder; check off what you did and schedule those things that you still need to do. You may get impatient if you don't see change right away. Remember to focus on your inner space, not just the outer. Be patient and confident. Connect with the power of balanced Wood as you move forward with courage and purpose.

The Fire Element

If you are Fire, you are probably inspired by what you've learned about yourself and your home. Now is the time to make some simple, quick changes to your home and invite some friends over to share your inspiration. Please share the ideas in this book with them! But in your enthusiasm to accomplish things now, don't forget to also do some of the inner work, meditations, spend time in nature, etc. Feel the vitality and warmth that balanced Fire brings into your life and those around you!

The Earth Element

If you are Earth, you may be feeling that you shouldn't spend so much time on yourself! Believe me, it is the most important thing. How can you help others if you are not operating from a more balanced place yourself? You may be a bit worried about making changes in your home and your life. You know that you need to do this, but may feel overwhelmed. Make the commitment to yourself and enlist the aid of a good friend to help you determine what changes you will implement first. Feel the power of balanced Earth, as it gently but firmly supports you and everyone around you.

The Metal Element

If you are Metal, you probably need some time to think through the changes first and carefully review the content. What suggestions make sense to you and what do not? Then, you will probably want to form a plan and prioritize what to do first. Take it slow and know that with your inner confidence and sincerity, you will create the harmony you are craving. Feel the power of Metal as it reconnects and realigns you to the sacred seed deep within.

The Water Element

If you are Water, you will probably need to take some time to digest what you have learned from this book and find your inspiration to make some changes. You may use some of the recommendations I've listed in this book, but you also may come up with some new creative, imaginative, out-of-the-box ideas to help you to envision subtle changes in your life and home. Then you will feel the deep power of Water as it flows effortlessly in your life!

DAILY TIPS FOR STRESS

This work is not magic. If you really want more harmony and joy in your life, you need to remember that it is as much an *inner* as an *outer* job. Creating a more harmonious home allows you to receive more positive energy in your life, but you have to be open to it and develop flexible chi and grow into the strengths of your True Nature. You have to be willing to flow with changing patterns of thought and behavior that may have become deeply ingrained over the years.

Stress often tells us that we are not in harmony with our True Nature Element. It may also point to an imbalance of at least one of the Five Elements. As you read through each of the Element chapters, hopefully you identified an Element that takes over when you are stressed out. We are all creatures of habit! For instance, my core Elements are Wood and Fire, but when I am stressed out, I usually become inflexible, highly critical, and need to control everything, which is a Metal imbalance. A great stabilizer for me is being observant of my breath or taking time to observe the changing sky—both Metal remedies.

Here are some tips to help when you get stressed:

Tip 1: Stop and Breathe

When you start feeling anxious and stressed out, please stop yourself. Moving faster to accomplish all those things we "need" to do doesn't improve the situation. It only makes us feel more frazzled, and then we make mistakes and create more problems. Instead, take a brief walk outdoors or just sit for a few minutes and breathe.

Tip 2: Mindfulness

Bring mindfulness into your daily life. Stop yourself and look out the window. I guarantee that you'll notice something that will bring a smile to your face. My desk is perpendicular to a large window. (Of course, I sit in command position with a full view of the room.) As I write the chapters in this book, I notice when my body is tense, my muscles need to stretch, and my eyes need to rest. Looking at a computer screen for hours at a time is very bad for vision—and not just physical vision, but inspired vision. I often raise my gaze to look out the window, regardless of weather or time of day. And sometimes, I am gifted with the most fantastic sunset that has snuck up totally unexpected as I am immersed in my writing. Or I watch as a soft breeze blows through the branches and leaves of the trees. And I give gratitude for that.

Tip 3: Awareness

Be aware of your energy and how it affects everyone around you. By using the tools in this book, you can make small positive changes to your home and lifestyle. You start a positive energetic shift that will spiral outward, enhancing your life and those around you. I know this to be true from my own life experience!

Tip 4: Restore

It is my sincerest hope that learning about nature and the Five Elements inspires you to become more aware of the natural world around you. We are so easily distracted by the bombardment of advertising, social media, and popular culture. We find it so easy to say, "I don't have time to walk in the woods," even though we know that doing just that can actually help us process challenges and make us feel so much more joyful and alive. How can we have time to walk through the mall and not the woods? Remember this: Make it a point to schedule some time in nature.

Believe me, I have had many consultations and I see how most clients love to do all the physical things in their spaces, but many never get to the *non*-physical recommendations, the sacred recommendations, such as journaling or meditation or spending time in nature. These remedies are often the most powerful.

Conclusion

By aligning your home and your life with your True Nature Element, you are allowing for a greater balance and harmony with your authentic self. This will let you achieve your highest goals and ignite your personal power in your daily life.

With these changes and an enhanced connection to nature you will be the beautiful person that you were meant to be. Joy can only emanate light—*lumen naturae,* the hidden light within. We are powerful beings, and our energy is powerful beyond measure. We often see how negative energy can pervade a group of people. Well, positive energy has the same impact. Expand that energy into your surroundings and life!

Connecting with the ways of nature can help you understand at a much deeper level what is going on inside of yourself—who you are and what your needs are—which is crucial to a higher level of consciousness. And when we raise our own consciousness, we help lift all of those around us. We add more light to the world, increasing the tiny bubbles that I saw in my dream journey with Archangel Gabriel overlooking the Earth. I saw those bubbles expand and take over the darkness. I saw it happen; therefore, it is already happening. You are a part of that. We all are.

Connecting with nature in your inner and outer spaces links the glimmer in your eyes to the golden shimmer of dawn.

Luminous Spaces Community

I hope you enjoyed learning about creating luminous spaces in your home and life.

Be sure to get your free download for an electronic version of the What Is Your True Nature? Assessment, MP3s of meditations and visualizations, and more at *luminous-spaces.com*.

And join in the conversation on our Facebook page: "Luminous Spaces Feng Shui." Please join this soulful community and share your thoughts and questions as well as your inspiration and experiences with this book. I am on there often and will connect with you.

How else can you help to expand the light in your world? Please share this book with friends. Organize a group to work with the ideas, or introduce it to your book club. Visit my website (to download the Book Club Kit that will spark interesting, life- and joy-enhancing conversation among your friends. There are so many ways to expand the light! I look forward to playing my part.

Share the Love on Social Media! Share your favorite quotes or ideas from this book on Facebook, Twitter, Pinterest, or Instagram. Use the hashtag #myluminousspace to help spread the word!

And finally, I have tremendous gratitude to all of you who have read this book. I see this as one of many movements in the right direction . . . toward the love, compassion, and joy that we are all entitled to in this life. We have chosen to be here at this major shift in consciousness. You are one of the awakened and are charged to give a strong, persistent nudge toward higher energy and consciousness. Let us all be the "cure," the light that radiates outward.

Enjoy your True Nature!   *Namaste, Maureen*

Acknowledgments

The amount of work that is required to conceptualize and write a book and then have it published is immense. No book is written alone. I want to thank all of those that have helped me birth this baby!

First, I want to thank my literary friend Cathy Judd (Metal Element) for her feedback on my writing. She gave me the courage to develop my own style and inspired confidence to reach out to bigger platforms.

Thanks to my friend and colleague, Dr. Jennifer Howard (Water Element), who spent many a breakfast meeting over the course of the last nine years hearing me talk about this book. She encouraged me and illustrated for me, through the writing and publishing of her own book, how persistence and dedication really pay off.

To my book coach, Suzanne Boothby (Water Element), who helped me write and rewrite the outline for this book and gave me invaluable feedback. Without her, my concept for this book would still be clear as mud. And thanks to my client, Christine Egan (Wood Element), for connecting me to the talents of Suzanne!

Thanks to my feng shui teachers and mentors, especially Alex Stark, who opened me to the shamanic perspective of reality, which has had a profound effect on my life. And thanks to my very first feng shui and five element teacher and mentor, Katherine Metz, whom I shared my outline and book concept with a couple of years ago. Her strong Metal gave me the direct feedback that was required and delivered it with such grace and compassion, as to awaken me to reposition the book to where it is today. She also inspired me to use my business name for the title (Luminous Spaces!).

I must thank all my consulting clients, especially those that have permitted me to share their stories in this book. Without them I would have no story to tell, no understanding on the inner workings of how we relate to our homes. Each consultation has uncovered more of the invisible reality that is our lives. Their collective experiences have provided the foundation to my work and have molded my philosophy of life.

A big thank you to my feng shui students for nearly a decade. Your confidence and soulful enthusiasm for this work have been the fuel to my fire! I am so grateful to have attracted a wonderful group of souls that are now part of my world and the feng shui community. I have learned as much from you as you have learned from me!

Thank you to my editor, Christine LeBlond (Metal Element), who believed in this book even when it wasn't quite there yet. Her kind guidance and support have been unrelenting throughout this process and have contributed much to this book!

And thanks to the staff at Red Wheel/Weiser who have enthusiastically taken my book under their very expert and professional wings. They provided wonderful guidance and support all along the way.

To Christine Keller (Fire and Water Elements), a childhood friend, who introduced me to an entirely unfamiliar and fascinating world of connectedness and meaning through Buddhism, dreams, and mysticism. She suggested I read Richard Louv's book *The Last Child in the Woods*, which facilitated the foundation of this book—that we need and *must* connect to the natural world.

To all of my childhood friends, I treasure you all and always: Michael Della Ragione, Caroline Quartuccio, Lynn Fisk, Antonet Bayrak, Laura Evans, Therese Coppola, and Betty Palumbo. You guys are my grounding, but most of all, my laughter and sense of belonging!

To my sister Pat Matheson. She is always there at my side when I have needed to unload or share some great news. I know that she is there and will provide whatever the occasion calls for. She is my rock (yes, she's Earth!) and is enthusiastically my biggest cheerleader! My big sis! And to my big brother Mike Matheson (also Earth) who has been both a gentle and strong support throughout my life.

To my loving and nurturing parents, Robert and Dorothy, who both in their living and death awakened me to the beauty of my spiritual path and purpose in life.

My children, Allison (Fire Element) and Bobby (and yes, Fire Element), who taught me how to transform and recover my True Nature. Through our lives together, I learned how to restore balance and harmony within and learned how to truly practice what I preach. These powerful experiences made me who I am today and for that I am truly grateful!

To my husband of thirty-two-plus years, Joe (Earth Element). At once we are the same crazy kids we were when we first met, but we are better! Exceedingly rare for couples, we traveled very different spiritual paths but wound up in the same spot. You really "get" me and I'll never forget what you said when I told you that I was writing this book. You said, "Of course!" You always told me to have confidence in my abilities, to never doubt myself, and never look to others thinking that they have it right. You have made me feel strong and solid in my own intuitive knowing and have participated on this wondrous spiritual journey of life! Learning more each day!

And lastly, to Archangel Gabriel for your encouragement and inspiration when I was at a loss on how to get my thoughts on paper. Through my dreams and visions, your Divine guidance was loud and clear.

Much Love & Blessings to All!
Maureen (Wood & Fire)

Appendix

The following charts are summaries of the Five Element content within the book for you to refer to as you discover your True Nature Element and learn what you can do within your home to support it. Refer to these charts to help.

CHART 1: LIST OF ELEMENT ATTRIBUTES

Below are some key terms for each of the Five Elements. You can use them to find the words that resonate with you for determining your True Nature Element in part three.

Wood—The Pioneer

Endurance	New beginnings	Thriving
Leadership	Growth	Self-sufficient
Loves challenge	Strength and	Action, initiative
Competitive	flexibility	Anger, frustration
Courageous	Lush	Impatient
Does well under	Green	Benevolent
pressure	Shade	Intolerant
Requires novelty	Good	Reckless
Action-oriented	Sustenance	Bored with
Great initiative	Vibrant	follow-through
Flexible	Leader	Arrogant
Adaptable	Visionary	Impulsive
Resilient	Confidence	Erratic behavior
Quick thinker	Branching out	Devious
Clever	Boundless	Ambivalence
Resourceful	Stability	Hates feeling
Breaks rules	Resilient	constrained
Spring	Rooted	Requires freedom
Sprouting	Blooming	

Fire—The Wizard

Communicative	Clarity	Speakers
Charismatic	Enthusiasm	Performers
Extrovert	Intuitive	Great at motivating
Sees the big picture	Follows gut instinct	others
Visionary	Inspires	Generous

Summer
Hot
Boisterous
Light
Warmth
Fun
Spontaneous
Excitement
Energy
Transforming
Formless
Burning
Boundless
Assertive
Guiding

Life of the party
Tempering
Temperamental
Consuming
Romantic
Heart
Flickering
Passionate
Raging
Hypnotizing
Compassionate
Destructive
Death/rebirth
Intense
Magic

Attractive
Performing
Dominating
Joy
Frenzy
Illuminating
Lighting the way
Anxious/panicky
Doesn't know how
   to pace himself
Burns out quickly
Overwhelmed
Bored with details
Requires coolness

Earth—The Peacemaker

Responsible
Reliable
Stable
Patient
Committed to goals
Sympathetic
Poised
Attentive
Assembles others
Service to others
Negotiator
Mediates
Creates environment
   of trust
Early fall
Mother Earth

Stability
Grounding
Nurturing
Home
Wanting peace
Sacrifice
Negotiate
Empathetic
Provider
Absorbing
Fruitful
Giving
Bountiful
Embracing
Forgiving
Unconditional

Resilient
Sentimental
Supportive
Resourceful
Loving
Seeking harmony
Worry
Contentment
Can get stuck
Averse to/ignores
   conflict
Hates change
Meddlesome
Conforming
Wishy-washy
Self-sacrifice

Dependent
Unrealistic
Issues with
  boundaries

Victim mentality
Smothering
Low self-esteem
Martyr syndrome

Enables/
  codependent
Unable to accept
  love/support

Metal—The Alchemist

Organizer
Creates structure
  from nothing
Methodical
Discerning
Calm
Disciplined
Great
  follow-through
Precise
Detail-oriented
Respects authority
Reasonable
Logical
Holds self and
  others to highest
  standard
Late fall
Natural leader
Letting go
Strategic

Grief, sadness
Controlling
Father figure
Judgmental
Decisive
Analytical
Seeks order
Cold
Precision
Always right
OCD
Opinionated
Sharp dresser
Integrity
Respect
Rule follower
Punctual
Unforgiving
Control
Precious
Refinement

Ritual
Sacred seeker
Self-critical
Perfectionist
Domineering
Uptight
Self-righteous
Austere
Formal
Petty
Compliant to a
  fault
Black/white
  thinking
Hypersensitive to
  environment
Hypocritical
Dislikes change
Unable to see the
  big picture

Water—The Philosopher

Great thinker
Curious
Imaginative
Creative

Independent
Introvert
Careful
Thrifty

Sensible
Playful
Articulate
Clever

Self-sufficient
Analytical
Conceive
Seeks knowledge
Seeks truth
Goes with flow
Most yin
Stillness
Quiet
Winter
Introspective
Rejuvenation
Flow
Mutable
Takes shape of
    container
Deep feelings,
    emotions

Cleansing
Imagination
A drop
Icy, steamy
Unstoppable
Impervious
Transformative
Cannot compress
Calming
Reflective
Roaring
Tumultuous
Darkness
Deep, shallow
Life
Saturated
Fear
Mysterious

Dreamer
Blunt
Withdrawn
Critical
Detached
Suspicious
Demanding
Unforgiving
Cynical
Preoccupied
Eccentric
Distrustful
Insecure
Requires warmth/
    heat

CHART 2: ELEMENT STRENGTHS
AND WEAKNESSES

Here is a recap of the strengths and weaknesses of each Element for easy reference.

Wood—The Pioneer (Chapter 5)

Strengths—Endurance, leadership, seeks and loves challenge and competition, courage, does well under pressure, requires novelty, action-oriented, great initiative, flexible and adaptable to challenges, resilient, quick thinking on their feet, clever and resourceful, breaks rules.

Weaknesses—Intolerance, recklessness, impatience, boredom with follow-through, arrogance, volatile emotions such as frustration and anger, impulsivity, erratic behavior, deviousness, ambivalence, abuse of stimulants and sedatives, hates feeling constrained.

Fire—The Wizard (Chapter 6)

Strengths—Communication, charisma, extrovert, great at assembling a team to fill in his gaps, has vision, often has great clarity on the end goal, great enthusiasm, very intuitive, follows hunches, great inspirer, speaker, performer, great at motivating others, generous.

Weaknesses—Can become anxious, doesn't know how to pace himself, may burn too brightly and then collapse (burnout), not a good planner, can be overwhelmed/become bored with details and follow-through, flirtatious.

Earth—The Peacemaker (Chapter 7)

Strengths—Responsible, reliable, grounded, stability, patient, commitment to goals, sympathetic, poised, attentive, assemble others, service to others, good at negotiation, mediates conflict, gives/

receives support from others, talented at achieving the most coop-eration with least sacrifice, creates environment of trust.

Weaknesses—Can get stuck (mud), not comfortable in leader-ship role, aversion to/often ignores conflict, insecure, does not like change, meddlesome, worried, conforming, scattered, wishy-washy, self-sacrifice, dependent, can be unrealistic, issues around personal boundaries, victim mentality, can be smothering, low self-esteem, martyr syndrome, enabler in codependent relationships, unable to accept love and/or help.

Metal—The Alchemist (Chapter 8)
Strengths—Leadership, planning, organizing, creating structure from nothing, methodical, discerning, calm, disciplined, great with follow-through, precise, detail-oriented, respects authority, reason-able, logical, holds self and others to the highest standard.

Weaknesses—Self-critical, perfectionist, domineering, uptight, self-righteous, austere, formal, petty, needs guidelines and rules, compliant to a fault/unable to break rules, needs control, black or white thinking, extreme sensitivity to environment, hypocritical, dislikes change, unable to see the big picture.

Water—The Philosopher (Chapter 9)
Strengths—Great thinker, curious, imaginative, creative, inde-pendent, introvert, careful, thrifty, sensible, playful, articulate, clever, self-sufficient, analytical, seeks knowledge and truth, self-knowledge, can go with the flow.

Weaknesses—Difficulty with initiating, dreamer, blunt, with-drawn, fearful, critical, detached, suspicious, demanding, unforgiv-ing, cynical, preoccupied, eccentric, distrustful, anticipates pitfalls, insecure, introverted.

CHART 3: SUMMARY OF WAYS TO CONNECT TO THE FIVE ELEMENTS

	Wood	Fire	Earth	Metal	Water
			Overarching Principle: Activating the Senses		
Organizing Principles	Movement and Vitality	Illumination and Connection	The Middle Way	Shiny and Clear	Wabi Sabi and Flow
The Element Itself					
Indoor Spaces	Views of trees/plants, wood items, furnishings and finishes, plants, flowers, driftwood	Views of sun, candles, fireplace, lighting fixtures, lamps	Views of mountains, open landscapes, soil, rock, stone, crystals	Views of sky, pieces of metal, metal ornamentation, furnishings, finishes (stainless steel, wrought iron)	Views of water, fountains, aquariums, container of water
Outdoor Spaces	Gardens, landscaping, wood fencing, gate, arbor, trellis, furniture	Fire pit, candles, lighting, pagoda, pyramid	Stone paths, patio, edging, seating, rock garden, statues, boulders	Metal structures, arbor, trellis, furniture, sculpture, ornaments	Natural bodies of water, pool, pond, hot tub, birdbath, waterfall
Symbols of Nature					
Materials & Fabrics	Plant-based fabrics (i.e., bamboo, cotton, linen, burlap)	Animal-based fabrics (fur, leather)	Granite, clay, slate, ceramic, terracotta, brick, raw stone; flannel, tweed, chenille, velvet fabrics	Brass, bronze, silver, coins, polished stone and marble; silk, metallic fabrics	Glass, mirror, shells, coral; sheer, chiffon fabrics

Color	Green	Red, purple, magenta, pink, deep orange	Beige to browns, yellow, peach, coral	White, off-white, gold, silver, gray, pastels	Black, blue
Shapes	Vertical, columnar, stripes	Triangle, pyramid, star, conical	Square, rectangle, horizontal lines	Round, oval, circular, arches, domes	Free-form, flowing, curves
Images/Artwork	Trees, plants, flowers	People, animals, fire, sun, star, desert	Open landscapes, mountains	Open sky, metallic finishes	Waterscapes, moon
Chi of Element	Initiative and vision, spontaneity and change, bold and direct	Connection, warmth and fun, drama, lights others up	Grounded and stable, proper boundaries, nourishment, the center	Structure and organization, simplicity, beauty and refinement, sacred	Flowing, playful and imaginative, quiet space
Other	Smell, sound of wind stirring trees	Sound of crackling fire, pets, wildlife	Smell of soil	Smell, sound of air/breeze	Smell, sound of water, rain
Connect in Nature	Forest bathing, work in the garden, sunrise, spring	Observe the sun, enjoy a fire/candle, noontime, summer	Work in garden, walk barefoot, climb a mountain, late afternoon, late summer	Observe weather or night sky, feel the wind, early evening, late autumn	Immerse in water, water sounds, viewing water, walk during rain, visit the ocean/negative ions, midnight, winter
The Sacred	Connecting to the Trees; Tree Meditation	Fire Meditation	Observing the Energy of the Land; Dowsing Exercise; Quartz Crystal Meditation	Space Clearing and Blessing Ritual; a Breath Meditation; Connecting Heaven and Earth Meditation	Create a Dream Journal; Dream Work Exercise; Purifying Bath Meditation

Bibliography

ENERGY AND CONSCIOUSNESS

Borland, C., and G. Landreth III. "Improved quality of city life through the Transcendental Meditation program: Decreased crime rate." In *Scientific Research on the Transcendental Meditation Program: Collected Papers* (vol. 1), 639–48, edited by D. W. Orme-Johnson and J. T. Farrow. Rheinweiler, Germany: Maharishi European Research University Press, 1976.

Conroy, Dr. Jim, and Basia Alexander. *Live and Let Live: How Multidimensional Collaboration Heals Ecosystems.* Morris Plains, NJ: Plant Kingdom Communications, LLC, 2014.

Emoto, Dr. Masaru. *The Hidden Messages of Water.* Hillsboro, OR: Beyond Words Publishing, 2004.

Hawkins, David R., MD, PhD. *Power vs. Force: The Hidden Determinants of Human Behavior.* Carlsbad, CA: Hay House, 1995.

Hay, Louise. *You Can Heal Your Life.* Carlsbad, CA: Hay House, 1984.

Howard, Dr. Jennifer. *Your Ultimate Life Plan: How to Deeply Transform Your Everyday Experience and Create Changes That Last.* Pompton Plains, NJ: New Page Books, 2012.

Linn, Denise, *The Secret Language of Signs: How to Interpret the Coincidences and Symbols in Your Life.* New York: Ballantine Books, 1996.

McTaggart, Lynne. *The Field: The Quest for the Secret Force of the Universe.* London: HarperCollins Publishers, 2001.

Mitchell, Edgar. *The Way of the Explorer: An Apollo Astronaut's Journey Through the Material and Mystical Worlds.* Franklin Lakes, NJ: Career Press, 2008.

Tompkins, Peter, and Christopher Bird. *The Secret Life of Plants: A Fascinating Account of the Physical, Emotional, and Spiritual Relations Between Plants and Man.* New York: Harper & Row, 1974.

Wohlleben, Peter. *The Hidden Life of Trees: What They Feel, How They Communicate, Discoveries from a Secret World*. Vancouver: Greystone Books, Ltd., 2015.

NATURE, PHILOSOPHY & SPIRITUALITY

Fisher, Mary Pat. *Living Religions*. Upper Saddle River, NJ: Prentice-Hall, 1991.

Louv, Richard. *The Last Child in the Woods*. Chapel Hill, NC: Algonquin Books, 2005.

Louv, Richard. *The Nature Principle: Reconnecting with Life in a Virtual Age*. Chapel Hill, NC: Algonquin Books, 2011

Moss, Nan, with David Corbin. *Weather Shamanism: Harmonizing Our Connection with the Elements*. Rochester, NY: Bear & Company, 2008.

Moss, Robert. *Dreamgates: An Explorer's Guide to the Worlds of Soul, Imagination, and Life Beyond Death*. New York: Three Rivers Press, 1998.

Picken, Stuart D. B. *Shinto Meditations for Revering the Earth*. Berkeley: Stone Bridge Press, 2002.

Redfield, James. *The Celestine Prophecy: An Adventure*. New York: Warner Books, Inc., 1997.

Somé, Malidoma Patrice. *Of Water and the Spirit: Ritual, Magic, and the Initiation in the Life of an African Shaman*. New York: Penguin Books, 1994.

Wilhelm, Richard, and Cary F. Baynes, trans. *The I-Ching: Or Book of Changes*. Princeton: Princeton University Press, 1967.

Wing, R. L. *The I-Ching Workbook*. Garden City, NY: Doubleday & Company, 1979.

FENG SHUI, FIVE ELEMENTS

Beinfield, Harriet, and Efrem Korngold. *Between Heaven and Earth: A Guide to Chinese Medicine*. New York: Ballantine Books, 1992.

Butler-Biggs, Jane. *Feng Shui Fusion: A Seasonal Guide to Good Energy*. New York: The Ivy Press, 2002.

Haner, Jean. *The Wisdom of Your Face: Change Your Life with Chinese Face Reading*. Carlsbad, CA: Hay House, 2008.

Haner, Jean. *Your Hidden Symmetry: How Your Birth Date Reveals the Plan for Your Life*. Carlsbad, CA: Hay House, 2013.

Kingston, Karen. *Creating Sacred Space with Feng Shui: Learn the Art of Space Clearing and Bring New Energy into Your Life.* New York: Broadway Books, 1997.

Kyriacou, Christian. *The House Whisperer: Discovering Your Relationship with the Heart of the Home.* Kingston upon Thames, UK: Ki Signature Books, 2014.

Linn, Denise, *Sacred Space.* New York: Random House. 1995.

BIOPHILIC DESIGN AND ARCHITECTURE

Alexander, Christopher, Sara Ishikawa, and Murray Silverstein. *A Pattern Language: Towns, Buildings, Construction.* Oxford, UK: Oxford University Press, 1977.

Browning, William, Catherine Ryan, and Joseph Clancy. "14 Patterns of Biophilic Design: Improving Health and Wellbeing in the Built Environment" (white paper). New York: Terrapin Bright Green, 2014.

Day, Christopher. *Places of the Soul: Architecture and Environmental Design as a Healing Art.* Tunbridge Wells, UK: Gray Publishing, 2002.

Kellert, Stephen. *Building for Life: Designing and Understanding the Human-Nature Connection.* Washington, DC: Island Press, 2005.

Kellert, Stephen. *The Good in Nature & Humanity: Connecting Science, Religion, and Spirituality with the Natural World.* Washington, DC: Island Press, 2002.

Kellert, Stephen, Judith H. Heerwagen, and Martin L. Mador. *Biophilic Design: The Theory, Science, and Practice of Bringing Buildings to Life.* Hoboken, NJ: John Wiley & Sons, 2008.

McHarg, Ian. *Design with Nature.* Garden City, NY: Doubleday/Natural History Press, 1969.

Sternberg, Esther M., MD *The Balance Within: The Science Connecting Health and Emotions.* New York: W.H. Freeman, 2001

Sternberg, Esther M., MD *Healing Spaces: The Science of Place and Well-Being.* Cambridge, MA: The Belknap Press, 2009.

PSYCHOLOGY: ENVIRONMENTAL PSYCHOLOGY AND ECOPSYCHOLOGY

Augustin, Sally. *Place Advantage: Applied Psychology for Interior Architecture.* Hoboken, NJ: Wiley, 2009.

Campbell, Joseph. *Myths to Live By: How We Re-Create Ancient Legends in Our Daily Lives to Release Human Potential.* New York: The Viking Press, 1972.

Cooper Marcus, Clare. *House as a Mirror of Self: Exploring the Deeper Meaning of Home.* Berkeley: Conari Press, 1995.

Macy, Joanna, and Molly Young Brown. *Coming Back to Life: Practices to Reconnect Our Lives, Our World.* Berkeley: New Society Publishers, 1998.

Roszak, Theodore. *The Voice of the Earth: An Exploration of Eco-Psychology.* Grand Rapids, MI: Phanes Press, 1992.

About the Author

Photo by Michele Kats

Maureen Calamia is a feng shui consultant, teaches a feng shui professional certification program, and is a board member of the International Feng Shui Guild. An inspiring thought leader in feng shui, energy, and consciousness, Maureen helps her clients and students integrate balance and harmony with their inner natures and their outer world. She merges the wisdom of feng shui and geomancy with biophilia and our need to be truly connected to the natural world for joy and well-being. Maureen has written for *Huffington Post, Elephant Journal, MindBodyGreen,* and *OmTimes Magazine.* She lives in St. James, NY. Visit Maureen at *luminous-spaces.com* and follow her @maureencalamia.

To Our Readers

Conari Press, an imprint of Red Wheel/Weiser, publishes books on topics ranging from spirituality, personal growth, and relationships to women's issues, parenting, and social issues. Our mission is to publish quality books that will make a difference in people's lives— how we feel about ourselves and how we relate to one another. We value integrity, compassion, and receptivity, both in the books we publish and in the way we do business.

Our readers are our most important resource, and we appreciate your input, suggestions, and ideas about what you would like to see published.

Visit our website at *www.redwheelweiser.com* to learn about our upcoming books and free downloads, and be sure to go to *www.red wheelweiser.com/newsletter* to sign up for newsletters and exclusive offers.

You can also contact us at *info@rwwbooks.com*.

Conari Press
an imprint of Red Wheel/Weiser, LLC
65 Parker Street, Suite 7
Newburyport, MA 01950
www.redwheelweiser.com